MIREILLE JOHNSTON'S

··

FRENCH
COOKERY
COURSE

PART ONE

MIREILLE JOHNSTON'S

••••••••••••••••••••••••••••••••

FRENCH
COOKERY
COURSE

PART ONE

BBC BOOKS

This book is published to accompany the
television series entitled *A Cook's Tour of France*
which was first broadcast in October 1992. The series was
produced by Clare Brigstocke.

Published by BBC Books,
a division of BBC Enterprises Limited,
Woodlands, 80 Wood Lane
London W12 0TT

Hardback and paperback First Published 1992
© Mireille Johnston 1992
Hardback ISBN 0 563 36768 7
Paperback ISBN 0 563 36309 6
Designed by William Mason
Recipes copy-edited and tested by Hilaire Walden

Photograph credits
Food photography by James Murphy. All other photographs by
David South except: Flassan, Provence; Vaucluse, Provence;
Geraniums in Alsace; back yard in Provence (IMP/Marie Louise Avery);
rivers and canals, Burgundy; house and ducks, Burgundy
(IMP/William Mason)
Styling by Helen Payne
Home Economist Allyson Birch
Set in Baskerville by Redwood Typesetting Ltd
Printed and bound in Great Britain by Clays Ltd, St Ives, Plc
Colour separation by Technik Ltd, Berkhamsted
Jacket and cover printed by Clays Ltd, St Ives Plc

CONTENTS

....

ACKNOWLEDGEMENTS

This book was prepared in connection with the BBC television series filmed by Clare Brigstocke and her merry crew in six regions of France. I want to express my gratitude to Clare whose indomitable energy and vision kept it and us all together.

Many thanks to Jenny Stevens for her confidence, Diane Hadley for her ever-present support, David South, Eric Fever, Michael White-house, and Mal Maguire for their superb work and their good spirits all along. Working with such a crew transformed hard work into a true pleasure.

I want to thank affectionately Suzanne Webber, my editor who has been constantly generous and attentive, Deborah Taylor for her patience, Hilaire Walden for her precision, Frank Phillips for his eye, and Khadija for her grace under pressure.

In the making of this series I want to acknowledge all the help we have received from SOPEXA, London and particularly from Gabrielle Allen who provided so many contacts and gave so much of her time. I also want to thank the many regional Chambers of Commerce and Tourist Committees, both regional and departmental, for their invaluable help during the research trips, and most especially the Pont l'Abbé Tourist Office.

I would also like to thank Eric du Chatellier and Patricia Rio at the Château de Kernuz Quimper for their kind cooperation during the demonstration filming.

And finally I want to thank all the people who during the filming welcomed us so warmly in their restaurants, in their homes, and shared with us their love for their region and its cooking:

RESTAURANT AUBERGE NANTAISE, *St Julien-de-Concelles*
THIERRY AND CHANTAL BALDINGER, *Lapoutroie*
RAYMOND AND SIMONE BONNOT, *Verdun-sur-Doubs*
ADOLPHE BOSSER, *Audierne*
FEDERATION OF CANTAL HUNTERS
HELENE CHARRASSE-MOINIER, *Entrechaux*
MARIE-JOSÉ COSSEC, *Pont-l'Abbé*
HOTEL d'EUROPE, *Morlaix*
THE FALDY FAMILY, *Roscoff*
JENNY FAJARDO DE LIVRY, *Fontvieille*
COLLET FALLER, *Klentzhelm*
THE GARDOT FAMILY, *Damvix*
SYLVIE KERSABIEC, *Moustoir-ac*
THE LAJUDIE FAMILY, *Chateau Chervix*
BERNARD LOISEAU, *Saulieu*
COMTE AND COMTESSE DU MANOIR DE JUAYE, *Champagne-la-Rivière*
RESTAURANT LA MARÉE, *La Rochelle*
JEAN-PIERRE MICHEL, *Fontvieille*
MICHEL MIOCHE, *Chamalières*
RENÉ AND MARCELLE DE MISCAULT LAPOUTROIE
JEAN-PIERRE MORIN, *Aurillac*
THE PELLISSIER FAMILY, *Peymeinade*
THE PERRIN FAMILY, *Sainte Croix en Bresse*
LULU PEYRAUD AND HER FAMILY, *Bandol*
ARMAND AND MONIQUE POINSOT *Arnay-le-Duc*
JEAN-FRANÇOIS RICHIN, *Louhans*
RESTAURANT LA SALAMANDRE, *Noirmoutier*
CLAUDE SIEGRIST AND HER FAMILY, *Beaune*

INTRODUCTION

••••••••••••••••••••••••••••••••

In Provence they sit under a linden tree and nibble an assortment of Petits Farcis; in Brittany, they eagerly await platters of golden Galettes; and in Auvergne a large bowl of steaming Truffade brings together three generations after a long but rewarding hunt for wild mushrooms. Whenever I am away from home, the memory of this kind of family Sunday lunch evokes France for me, the joy of conversation, the laughter and the pleasure of sharing a few lovingly prepared dishes.

Fair France and Fine Food Forever! We've all heard about it . . . and for so long that we almost take it for granted. But is it a marriage made in heaven or a period piece? Today, like the queen leaning towards her mirror, French Cuisine asks, 'Am I still the fairest of them all?' The proof of the pudding, of course, is in the eating, but the real question is, which pudding do we eat?

Many of the recipes I have gathered together in this book have been passed from generation to generation with improvements and additions on the way. They are a medley of old and new, classic and regional recipes we can all do in our kitchen today. Old classics such as *Truite au Bleu* (see p. 78), *Sole Meunière* (see pp. 84–5), *Choux à la Crème* (see pp. 210–11) along with more recently created recipes such as *Salade de Coquilles St Jacques* (see p. 107), *Huitres Chaudes* (see p. 105–6) and fragrant *Flan des legumes* (see p. 163). But the bulk of these recipes like *Daube aux Olives* (see p. 138), *Poule au pot farcie* (see pp. 114–16), and *Pauchouse* (see pp.70–71), have their roots in regional cookery, the patrimony of all serious food in France. Do not be surprised if you find no trendy Mousses, no dazzling spun sugar extravaganzas, truffle stuffed leeks, or preparations requiring a brigade of thirty apprentices and a chef.

In France, cookery remains one of the true, solid links uniting individuals and generations. While it is always taken seriously, it is not thought to require extraordinary reverence nor exceptional technical prowess. It is, instead, viewed as a gentle ritual which helps to hold families and friends together asserting its confident strength against all the tugging and pulling of changing times.

And the times, they are indeed changing in France with its quicker-is-better approach to technology from high-speed trains and Concorde, minitels and microwaves to frozen and vacuum-packed food. The average person has little time to shop and cook as he or she runs from home to work and back again. Yet food is one of the ways most people in France stay in touch with their family and regional roots. City dwellers still find the time to spot a fine melon, evaluate the crispness of an artichoke, the maturity of a brie or the freshness of a trout.

Chantal, in Roscoff, says there is little time for cooking when one has a job and a family, but as a good Breton, she has taught her children to gather mussels, clams and winkles. Her husband often brings back beautiful bass and bream from fishing trips and they're prepared for Sunday lunches, especially when her relatives visit. Of course, on these occasions she always manages to make her special flan with plenty of caramel or her *Oeufs à la Neige* with cooked apples. They are her mother's and daughter's favourites. She's not a scholarly cook. She does not think of herself as a chef. She just cooks as one breathes, without thinking about it, spontaneously. This is true for all of us, a meal need not be a fussy affair; with an attentive eye as we choose the ingredients, a serious recipe to guide us, we can all express in our cooking a convivial gesture with a warmth and ease that cannot be shared in any other way.

But if cooking is mostly about relating to people it is also about connecting with nature around us. I remember last summer, I had decided it was to be a lazy holiday: minimal cooking and no entertaining – my vegetable garden had other ideas. It suddenly started to produce basket after basket of courgettes: long grey ones and tiny green round ones. In response, I threw myself into a mad whirl making courgette soup, stuffed courgettes, courgette gratins, Ratatouille, courgette omelettes, courgette flans, courgette savoury tarts and more besides. I couldn't let the garden down; I couldn't ignore the firm, crisp vegetables. Caught in its rhythms, I became one with my garden and its harvest.

One thing my experience with the courgettes taught me is the importance of recipes. Without them, I wouldn't have a notion of what to do. Recipes, I find, are to pleasurable cooking what road maps are to travel. They get you there. The recipes in this book are as reliable and often as old as their region but every generation has added its own accent, and ours is no exception. Today, we tend to prefer the sharp refreshing taste of dandelion, watercress and chicory to reliable and bland lettuces. We enjoy meat and fish cooked so they retain their natural juices served in simple wine sauces thickened with carrot or onion purées, and Beurre Nantais, the pungent reduction of vinegar and shallots sauce, has replaced thick cream sauces for many of us. We eat a wide variety of vegetables prepared in a vast number of different ways: raw, stewed, steamed, puréed, in gratins and in timbales. We still love unctuous dishes like *Blanquette de Veau* (see pp. 134–5) or *Boeuf Bourguignon*

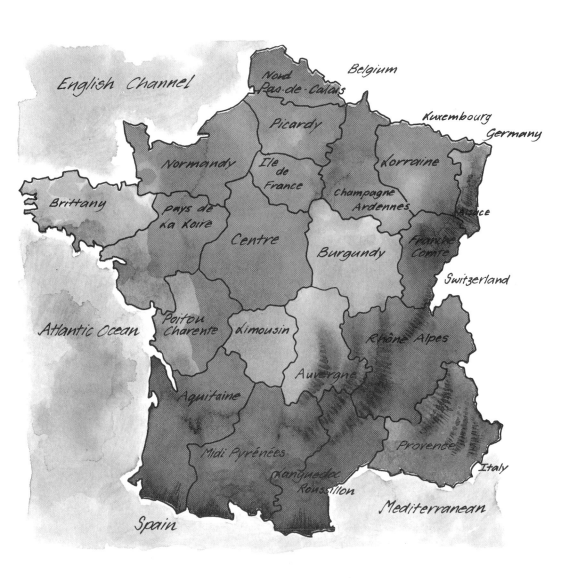

(see pp. 140–1) as long as most of the fat has been skimmed off and the sauce is accented with lemon and herbs. Olive oil is usually used to replace plain groundnut oil and traditional lard. And when we make cakes and custards, we may flavour them with bitter chocolate (see p. 184), lemon, ginger, coffee, orange or fruit brandy (see p. 193), *Gâteau Breton* (see p. 218) and *Madeleines* (pp. 212–13) are more frequently served with sliced oranges and Apple Compote. Fruit tarts (see pp. 202–9), fruit fritters (see p. 96), omelettes (see p. 197), and salads tend to replace the creamy heavier desserts.

But what truly determines the quality of our regular meals as well as our most ambitious feasts in France today is the growing and persistent demand in open air markets and supermarkets throughout the country for first-rate ingredients. A crusade for good quality products at reasonable prices led by stubborn consumers and ambitious chefs over the past twenty years has yielded visible results. They have been supported by oyster breeders in Loire Atlantique, vegetable farmers in the south, vignerons in Burgundy, cheese makers refining their mellow Chèvres for weeks and, in Auvergne, their crumbly Cantal for years, beekeepers producing fine honey in the Alps, shepherds driving their flocks of sheep for miles in search of good grass, cattle breeders in Limousin, Bresse farmers feeding milk and corn to their free-range poultry, charcutiers patiently curing and smoking their sausages – all of these artisans are fighting to preserve not only a livelihood but a heritage, and none is ready to see centuries of training and experience become obsolete.

Each of the six regions introduced in this book is defined by specific products, specific dishes with specific flavours. So, while many regions prepare their own versions of a classical dish such as *Coq au Vin* (see pp. 117–19) they will use sharp white wine in Alsace, a hearty red in Burgundy or a sweet white wine in Savoy. The chicken may be seasoned with orange rind and herbs in the South but accompanied by bacon and onions in Burgundy.

The recipes in this book are divided in seven parts: starters, fish, shellfish, poultry, meats, vegetables and desserts. Each recipe section has dishes from all the regions of France, even those not in the six regions introduced in this book. The recipe introductions include information and advice on how to select and prepare special ingredients as well as tips on how to save time. There are snippets about the cooks who have provided recipes for the television programme *A Cook's tour of France* and which I have sometimes adapted for this book.

Picasso's advice to his painter friends was, 'to draw you must close your eyes and sing'. This applies to all of us in our kitchens. Cooking is not ostentatious juggling with clumsy implements and finicky ingredients nor is it a scientific experiment. Cooking is an open process; there are no sacred rules. Remember Chantal; we must, like her, cook with appetite, confidence and without taking it too seriously. A good meal should not amaze or awe, it should offer a suspended moment of truce and pleasure to you and to your guests.

It was always felt that the hostess had to be calm and unruffled on the surface and frantic underneath like the duck paddling along, but this is no longer true. Many of the dishes in this book can be prepared in advance so with the shopping and most of the cooking done ahead of time there is little to do at the last moment. You will have time to remove the fat from a sauce or stew, trim the *Pot au feu* (see pp. 144–6) meats, organise your table, dress yourself calmly and then bring forth the meal with grace and without pressure.

These recipes are at the core of a way of living which all of us can master. They reflect the art of the possible that allows us to cook with what is at hand. We can, thanks to them, make the most of a plain cabbage, a bushel of clams and a basket of pears.

REGIONAL INTRODUCTIONS

BRITTANY

Brittany, with its silvery light and clouds scudding in from the open sea is a mysterious, dreamlike province softly coloured in greys and blues. But while those soft hues are the colours of dreams they are also those of the granite which this region is founded on and which symbolises the endurance of its people. Like their houses, their churches and monuments Bretons are made of granite. Between waves of invasion and plundering by barbarian tribes, medieval pirates and modern armies, nature has regularly dealt brutally with Brittany's farmers and fishermen. After each new catastrophe couples have joined together to salvage what they could of their livelihood, thus forging solid bonds. There is a Breton saying which reflects that solidarity between men and women: 'If the man earns the bread, it is the woman who churns the butter.'

Brittany's calm setting conceals great energy and powerful spiritual forces. Elaborate rites took place at Carnac as early as 200 BC when worshippers recreated the precise patterns based on astronomy in twenty-foot-high granite stones. Today, religion remains a priority. Bretons are the most serious believers in all of Catholic France with hundred of local saints. Brittany's dark dimension, its fascination with happenings beyond life's grey appearance has spawned fertile legends of King Arthur, Merlin the Sorcerer and Viviane, and doomed Tristan and Isolde as well as a host of other magicians, demons and saints.

Sculpted like a proud ship's bow, this lonely peninsula at Europe's western extremity, has moved for centuries to the rhythms of the sea. Brittany's stubborn and independent character makes it seem even more remote from the rest of France than it is. Hunters first settled in the area around 5000 years ago, but it was only when the Celts came from Britain that it became known as Little Britain, later Brittany. A powerful Duchy in the Middle Ages, Brittany formally joined the kingdom of France following a rapid succession of three royal weddings to French kings.

This misty peninsula yokes together powerful but contrary tendencies that fire the distinctive Breton energy. Divided culturally between French-speaking upper Brittany to the east, and lower Brittany, 'Bretagne Bretonnante', in the west where Breton dialect and traditions prevail, the region is also split into two geographically, between Armor and Argoat.

Armor is the 'country near the sea' with cliffs of pink and violet rocks high above the fishing villages and harbours. Every Breton is said to be born 'with sea water flowing around his heart'. St Malo, Roscoff, Brest, Quimper, Concarneau – every big city except for Rennes – is on the coast. There are 750 miles of coastline with sandy beaches, steep pink and blue granite cliffs, peaceful bays and small islands.

Inland is Argoat, 'the country near the woods', with its melancholy moors and woodlands, fields of ferns, old stones, soft hills and fresh green pastures. Here, the tidal rivers carry life-giving water to inland pastures and villages where camelias, mimosas, hydrangeas, apple, fig and palm trees stand in striking contrast to Armor's wind-battered coasts.

Brittany is France's most important fishing region, and everyone who lives near the coast is involved with it. Early in the morning, the return of the commercial fishing boats is followed by armies of optimistic seagulls and in ports such as Concarneau or Guilvinec most of the village attends 'la criée', the daily fish auction.

Typical of the region's cookery is *Crabes à la Mayonnaise* (see pp. 100–1), the *Assiette de Fruits de Mer* (see pp. 98–9), and *Moules et Palourdes Farcies* (see pp. 102–3). These recipes are a simple response to ingredients with such freshness and flavour that they need little elaboration. Noirmoutier's freshly gathered sea salt flavours the local fresh butter, and this beurre salé enhances everything in local cooking from a platter of little grey prawns to a *Gâteau Brêton* (see p. 218) as well as the beloved *Crêpes and Galettes* (see pp. 180–2) which still play a large part in meals in Brittany.

One of the most famous and indeed, controversial, of Brittany dishes is *Lotte à l'Armoricaine* (see pp. 86–7). The origin of this atypical dish is a topic of endless discussion which will probably never be resolved to everyone's satisfaction. But meanwhile the debate adds to the charm of eating the dish.

Chestnut and mistletoe have been Brittany's symbols for many centuries – chestnuts because before cereal crops grew in the region they were the basis of most meals, mistletoe because it is sacred and represents persistence.

Despite several oil spills on the coast, fierce tempests, and failed economic ventures, the new generation of Bretons no longer passively accepts a legacy of hardship and poverty. There is now a feeling that Brittany has entered the modern world without either betraying her past or selling short her future. She has elegant seawater spas in Quiberon, Roscoff, and St Malo; a proliferation of small industries harnessing native resources; Roscoff's efficient vegetable cooperative, a computerised

Above: Arcais in Deux-Sèvres on the Atlantic coast. The white houses and *bachots*, flat-bottomed boats, are typical of the region.

Previous page: Tending the oyster beds in Charente-Maritime on the Atlantic coast.

'Wall Street of Vegetables' sells and delivers the region's artichokes, cauliflowers and onions internationally.

Mysterious, traditional, bittersweet Brittany. No matter where I look – prim ladies with their lace and starched coifs turning crêpes on their griddles, fishermen pulling in their nets, dancers in the village square weaving their delicate steps – I see the same quiet, cheerful determination. But my favourite vision of Brittany today is the one that links the two lands of Argoat and Armor, the past and the future; a flight of graceful seagulls winging their way inland over fields of silvery artichokes.

THE RECIPES OF BRITTANY

••••••••••••••••••••••••••••••••••••••

Lotte à l'Armoricaine 86–7

Crabes à la Mayonnaise 100

Moules et Palourdes Farcies 102

Flans de Légumes 163

Crepes and Galettes 180

Omelette aux Pommes 197

Gâteau Breton 218

THE ATLANTIC COAST

Loire-Atlantique, Charentes-Maritime,

Deux Sèvres, Vendée

Stretching from flat Atlantic beaches towards the heart of France, Loire Atlantique evokes the best of provincial life, a blending of measure and pleasure. People here have always shared their land with water; draining marshes, digging canals and setting boulders to control the floods of the Loire. Marshes of the Marais Poitevin – Green Venice – have been converted into fertile gardens and pastures, and as we enter it we find ourselves in an enchanting world of narrow waterways lined with reeds, willows, elms and poplars. Punts and narrowboats with cows and sometimes an occasional plough on board, glide silently by on the green, sun-dappled water, beneath a canopy of trees.

Calm today, the region's past is filled with all manner of mayhem from plagues to bloody, religious wars to major battles as in 732 AD when Charles Marel turned back the Sarracens' invasion of Europe. Yet, for violence and emotion none of these matched the Vendée revolt that ripped the country apart in the French Revolution pitting Royalists against Republicans with columns of soldiers burning and looting the countryside. Typical of its passion is a short speech General de la Rochejacquelein made to his forces just before he led them into battle.

> If I advance, follow me!
> If I retreat, kill me!
> If I die, avenge me!

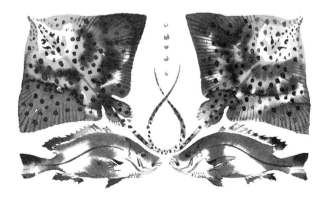

Serenity has replaced such turbulence. All along the Atlantic coast are golden beaches and gentle cliffs, beautifully tended oyster beds, and inland, just a few kilometres away, pastures enclosed by hawthorn hedges. There are moors and creeks, canals sheltered by trees, and vineyards on the banks of the Charentes river. This peaceful place is blessed with wild geese, ducks, woodcocks, dairy cows, goats, freshwater fish, and also more elusive creatures like eels, snails and frogs.

In this region, single-storey white houses abound. They usually have two main entrances – one for the back leading to the pasture, the other opening on to the front where a flat bottomed boat, a 'bachot', is often anchored on the waterway. Southwards are beautiful limestone houses, manors, castles, and abbeys of granite all of which seem to grow out of the hills as if they were part of them.

The island of Noirmoutier, just off the coast, is linked to the mainland by a causeway and offers mountains of sea salt, fields of potatoes, an array of delicate windmills, and pretty white houses with pink, blue and green shutters which often complement the colour of the owner's boat. The island sits at the mouth of the estuary of the Loire river. River banks have always belonged to fishermen, to bicycle riders, to couples lost in dreams and mostly to the celebrated 'guinguettes'. Many of these small bistros where farmers, city dwellers, and fishermen used to gather to drink local Muscadet wine, dance, sing and eat platters of frogs and eels are still there. Music and dancing have been replaced by the energetic bustle of winegrowers, businessmen, and families enjoying salmon or pike served with the famous Beurre Nantais, a deliciously delicate butter, shallot, and vinegar sauce that can transform any plain fish or vegetable into one of France's most tempting dishes.

ATLANTIC COAST

Cookery on the Atlantic Coast draws on exceptionally fine products. This is the home of celebrated and glorious brandy, Cognac. Pineau, the local alcoholic charmer, is a Cognac wine which is served as an aperitif. Here, you will find a great variety of spring vegetables including Charlotte potatoes, orange-fleshed Charentais melons and Marans chickens, as well as ducks, frogs, eels, snails (called 'lumas' or 'Cagouilles'), and Bulot mussels. Above all there are exceptionally luscious Marennes oysters, and the nutty-flavoured local butter, one of France's finest, as well as the local Gros Plant and Muscadet wines enhance it all.

The cookery of the region is slow – sometimes called 'cuisine de cagouillard', as if prepared at a snail's pace. The Chaudrée is a local white fish and garlic soup. Oysters may be served raw with crisp sausages and a glass of sweet Pineau or baked with cream and chopped leeks as *Huîtres Chaudes* (see pp. 105–6). Mussels are often stuffed, *Moules et Palourdes Farcies* (see p. 102), or prepared as *Moules marinières* (see pp. 104–5), or seasoned with wine and cream to become the glorious stew, Mouclade. Snails are cooked with garlic, wine, shallots, bacon, and mushrooms and duck is flavoured with apples, fresh grapes and Muscadet. Pike is stuffed with pork, ham is cured with sea salt, spices and brandy cider, and mojettes, white haricot beans, are cooked with herbs, tomato and ham (see p. 177). Farci Vendéen or Pouti is made with all a garden offers in the way of sorrel, Swiss chard, fresh herbs and cabbage. The delicate Crémets Nantais and Caillebotte are the lightest of milk desserts.

Patience is expressed in this region's pace of life whether it is in the breeding of lambs, mussels and oysters or in the cookery of traditional dishes. With the shimmering waters of the sea and waterways reflecting a pale sky, with fields of rich cereals and fresh vegetables and its orderly vineyards, the Atlantic Coast has definitely turned away from the temptations of her tumultuous past. It has taken to heart the poet Aragon's praise of the flowers' quiet refusal to bend to the winds of panic. Thus it is in the Loire-Atlantique that a flowering plant, a rose bush, is traditionally placed at the end of each row of Cognac vines to protect the precious crop from whatever might assail it.

THE RECIPES OF THE ATLANTIC COAST

••••••••••••••••••••••••••••••

ALSACE

At first sight, one is struck by the picturesque, fairy story, folksy charm of Alsace. There is an abundance of wrought-iron signs, grey-cobbled streets, covered bridges, half-timbered stucco houses and steepled roofs. It is a prim, quaint region exuding warmth and comfort. The houses all have window boxes and wooden balconies which overflow with brightly coloured geraniums. Inside, the rooms are dominated by the huge porcelain stoves, while brass and copper pans on the walls and majestic grandfather clocks all give a cosiness which is more than good enough to help its inhabitants face the bleakest of winter days.

More than any French region, Alsace's geography is the key to its past and future. Squeezed between the Rhine river and Vosges mountains, Alsace has been fought over by Germany and France since 300 BC when the Teutons first drove the Celts out of the area. It became part of Charlemagne's empire in the seventh century AD when his sons divided his empire and was Germany's until the 1500s. France's growing presence met resistance from a population accustomed to German rule until the French Revolution moved them to become so French in spirit that more than 50 000 Alsatians chose to settle in France when Germany took their land in 1871. The extraordinary life of a friend's grandfather illustrates this shifting of nationality between France and Germany which Alsace has experienced. He was born French in Alsace, became German in 1871, French in 1918, German in 1940. When he died in 1950, a citizen of France, he had changed nationality four times in his life.

Yet, as Alsace confronts the future, its geography and history, a curse for so long, may turn out to be a blessing that permits it to take full advantage of today's European, rather than national, perspective. With many trade and legal barriers disappearing, the only obstacles that will remain will be those of differing cultures and languages – obstacles with which Alsatians are at least equally familiar as any people in Europe.

Alsace's rich plain, nourished by the Rhine's alluvial soil, is the source of a wide variety of resources. It has oak and pine forests, orchards, pastures, cattle and game. There is the 'wine road' with its rows of perfectly tended vineyards, charming villages, ramparts and medieval castles perched on hilltops, and old churches of both the Catholic and Protestant denominations. The region has several large towns such as Colmar, Mulhouse, Ribeauville and of course Strasbourg, with its pink-stoned cathedral, which is both the home of the European Parliament and the region's capital.

With such a chaotic past, the Alsatians might have long ago lost their centre of gravity had they not drawn on their traditions to affirm the values they share. A multitude of traditional fairs and feasts are celebrated with elaborate pageantry. At these events women wear lavish costumes with huge black or red bows in their hair and parade through the streets accompanied by colourful bands, adorned carriages and the ringing of bells. Enthusiastic crowds flock to village festivals honouring patron saint and local produce; asparagus, trout, herring, walnuts, frogs, chitterlings, snails, gingerbread, beer, the grape harvest and, of course, the French version of Sauerkraut, la Choucroute.

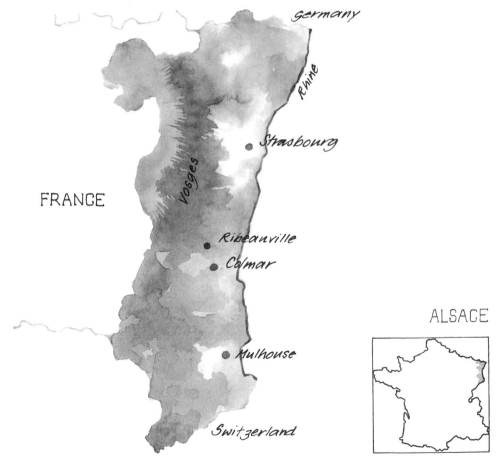

Keeping Alsatian traditions alive has necessitated keeping storks alive. A few years ago, storks, the bearers of good luck in Alsace, were placed on the endangered species list. Since then a sustained effort has been made throughout the region to make sure that storks were carefully bred, fed, and kept warm in winter. In their huge nests on top of chimneys, the proliferating storks are symbols for Alsatians not only of continuity with the past but also of the importance of working together today.

Gatherings, most often 'en famille' take place in bustling Tavernes on long wooden tables around a hearty *Baeckeoffe* (see pp. 146–7), a pyramidal *Choucroute garni* (see pp. 148–50) enriched with six or nine different dishes of meats or fish. But they also gather in Winstub bistrots where Riesling, Gewurztraminer, Sylvaner wines are served with herrings and cream, twisted egg noodles or crisp potato cakes *Galettes de Pommes de Terre* (see pp. 172–3). Of such abundance, they are proud to say, 'In France food is good, but there isn't much of it, in Alsace it is good, and there is plenty of it'.

Cookery in Alsace is based on local produce and recipes held in a collective memory which have been passed down through the ages. Even if freshwater fish, pork, wild berries, and game are no longer all to be found in Alsace itself it is still imported, and these basic ingredients are still prepared according to traditional recipes. Winemakers, bakers, pastry cooks, butchers, charcutiers – all these food artisans infuse new energy into the region's patrimony. In Colmar, I met the Helmstetters, father and son who are still following the recipes written down a century ago by Helmstetter the elder's great grandfather. The recipe book is beautifully adorned and written in gothic German. When we met they were baking some 500 different breads a day.

In Kayserberg, I met a butcher curing his fresh hams with coarse salt and spices, preparing more than 50 kinds of sausage with garlic, caraway seeds, aniseeds, cumin and pepper and smoking his charcuterie in a fragrant mixture of fruit woods.

In Lapoutroie, I sipped pear, mirabelle, holly berry, winebud, quince and wild berry brandies as well as Kirsch. I was told that this type of brandy is called 'eau de vie blanche' – 'white life water' – because, unlike Cognac, it ages in crockery rather than oak.

Everywhere I went I ate breads and cakes of all sorts: freshly baked pretzels; rye, wheat, barley, and 'Miesel' breads; apple, blueberry, raspberry and the local quetsch plum tarts (see p. 202); *Kugelhopf* (see p. 216), Stollen, spicy Bireweck, Anisbredle, Schwonebredle, Mandalbaebbe; and brightly decorated little gingerbread figures topped with crisp icing.

Alsace, on the threshold of being European, is perhaps the most environmentally sensitive and technologically oriented of regions. People here work hard in every field and in terms of food Alsatians are among the most innovative and competitive of chefs. They have transformed traditional hearty cookery recipes into an ambitious and refined cuisine and earned the region's restaurants a large number of highly-rated Michelin stars. But excellence in that field is also a part of their tradition. Alsace inspired France's most celebrated gourmet, Brillat Savarin to declare, 'It is one of the regions of France where I salivated the most'. Were he to return today, he would not change his mind.

AUVERGNE AND LIMOUSIN

Here we stand in the very centre of France, 'La France Profonde'. The volcanic landscape of the Massif Central with its quiet winding roads, serene medieval villages, sparkling creeks, and bounty of wild flowers is perhaps the most isolated, least spoiled region of France. It is also one of the most sparsely populated areas in Europe. Limousin has, in fact, more lambs than people.

Throughout this rugged province one finds a solid architecture of squat fortresses, sturdy castles and Romanesque churches topped with petal-shaped tiled roofs. Like its buildings, the extraordinary energy and character of Auvergne's people has been shaped by the region's austerity.

Here the truth of the old proverb 'The most important thing parents can give their children are roots and wings' is still observed as the motto of the region. In Auvergne parents endow their children with a sense of realism, independence and the courage to strike out on their own to make their fortunes. As a result, for centuries, Auvergnats left their homeland to seek a better life in Paris. Each autumn, after the herds had been driven down to the valleys, the wood cut and stacked, villagers would walk the hundreds of kilometres to Paris and work all winter at jobs no one else would do, carrying hot water to the top floors of hotels and apartments or selling and delivering coal and firewood. Stone masons from Auvergne, known as 'white sparrows', built such monuments as the Royal Palace of Versailles and the Louvre. In May, many of them would return home to take the cattle into the open fields and prepare for the summer crops.

In Paris, the most industrious of the Auvergnats stayed on to start small restaurants in the tiny rooms where coal and barrels of wine were usually stored. They began by serving their customers simple food; country-cured ham, dried sausages and an occasional cabbage soup. Over time, many of them turned their little shops into simple cafés and bistros which have since grown into brasseries and great restaurants. Many of the most formidable establishments in Paris, Le Dôme, La Coupole, le Flore, and Lipp were founded and run by Auvergnats, so that today Paris is still said to be Auvergne's largest village.

Marie and Baptiston, the traditional Auvergnat characters frequently appear in stories and songs inspired by the region's fierce determination to survive. These two figures are courageous, penny-pinching and depicted as always straining upwards on steep roads that never seem to turn into easy downhill paths. But, along the way, solid Auvergnat friends stand ready to support them if they falter: 'Si tu glisses, tends la main', 'If you slip, stretch out your hand.'

An extraordinary passion for agricultural excellence has always distinguished Auvergne and Limousin, and today they raise some of France's best lamb, veal and beef. Breeders and butchers have long been among the most powerful forces in this region. A single street in fourteenth century Limoges had 58 butchers with their own patron saint, St Aurelien, and a chapel, which today still belongs to their guild. Both the pale-caramel coloured Limousin cattle and the tall long-horned Salers cows, (which look as if they just stepped out of a pre-historic engraving) from Auvergne are superbly bred. In a highly competitive industry, farmers, breeders, and butchers all close ranks whenever it is necessary to preserve a standard that justifies the label Blason Prestige, a symbol of quality authenticating where and how each animal has been raised.

Because the winters are hard and the country is rugged, regional cookery relies on heartwarming dishes seasoned with cheese, pork fat, and walnut oil. Potatoes are known here as 'the truffles of the poor' and are the foundation of the beloved *Truffade* (see p. 176) which blends them with fresh local Tome cheese and to make a highly satisfying and fragrant dish. When garlic is added and the mixture is cooked so it is crisp, like a pancake, it becomes an Alicot, another favourite.

Other traditional dishes are also hearty, such as robust, warming soups, fragrant Potées and rich stews, especially of game such as *Chevreuil en Ragout* (see pp. 151–2). Wild mushrooms, like Ceps, are popular

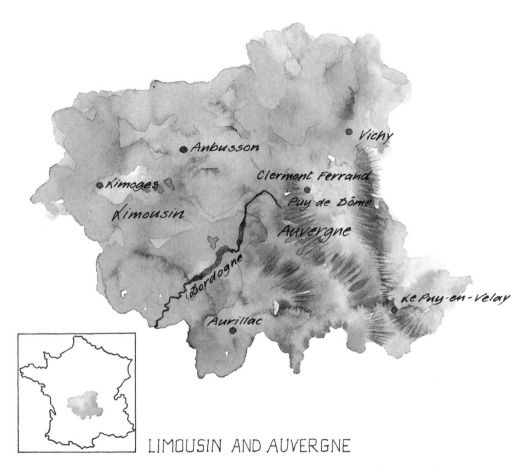

LIMOUSIN AND AUVERGNE

when seasoned with sautéed garlic and parsley (see p. 168 for *Cèpes Sautés*).

One delicate product of the region is a tiny green lentil from Le Puy which Michel Mioche combines in his *Saumon aux Lentilles* (see p. 79) with the freshwater salmon from local rivers and streams.

Apart from its fine meats and robust charcuterie, the region is proudest of its cheese. The cows graze on the steep hills covered with grass but also gentian, wild pansies and liquorice which give a distinctive flavour to the celebrated Cantal cheese. Cantal with its thick crust and crumbly texture is made in stone houses perched on the hills or in efficient cooperatives and then nurtured and aged for years in moist cellars. Some weigh up to 36 kilos. The region also produces high quality *tommes* and luscious Saint Nectaire. Blue cheeses like Bleu d'Auvergne and the Fourme d'Ambert are usually served with bread, and either fresh pears or a handful of walnuts. One of the most interesting dishes I tasted in Clermont-Ferrand was *Poires à la Fourme d'Ambert* (see p. 186). Favourite desserts in the region are the wild bilberry creamy custards and tarts and a large variety of walnut and chestnut cakes.

Auvergne is one of the rare regions in France which cannot boast any great wine but curiously it is a major supplier of bottled spring mineral waters. Rain water, filtered through rock and volcanic soil, springs forth in sources yielding more than 400 million bottles a year. Badoit, Vichy, and Volvic are just four names from a great variety of different types of bottled waters, countless springs and spas. There is at least one mineral water for every ailment involving the liver, obesity, kidneys, skin, and arteries.

The superb Aubusson tapestries, fine Limoges porcelain, Laguiole knives and of course Michelin tyres are also produced in the region. In addition to all this, Clermont-Ferrand, the capital, is the birthplace of the famous *Guide Michelin*.

In 1900, André Michelin decided to offer each of his customers a little red book with precious addresses of approved restaurants, accommodation and reliable garages for car repairs. A century later it has become the gourmet's bible. Every year, twelve Michelin inspectors anonymously visit restaurants throughout France keeping notes on each one and sharing impressions with their colleagues. At the end, a new hierarchy of excellence is announced; an event awaited with intense hope and anguish by chefs in every corner of France. Only nineteen restaurants in the whole of France are currently blessed with the three stars, Michelin's ultimate accolade.

What matters for Michelin is that the restaurants demonstrate a sustained commitment to quality. In recent years boutiques, swimming pools, helicopter pads, exquisite cutlery and gazebo-like dining rooms seemed to be given priority over food. There is now a return to more culinary values signalling that the *Guide Michelin* has remembered that it is a child of Auvergne.

It is often said that the region can be characterized as a place which offers 'volcanoes, cheeses, prime ministers and presidents of the republic'. Many volcanoes, at least seven great cheeses, and recently two prime ministers and two of France's last three presidents have come from this region and today on Clermont-Ferrand's main square, the statue of Vercingetorix, a native son and the leader of the Gauls, is mounted on his

Above: Flassan, Provence. The small windows with their blue and green shutters, which help to keep houses cool in the heat of the day, are a common feature of the region.

Previous page: The coloured tiles on the roof of the Hospice de Beaune in Burgundy are a fine example of this regional architectural feature.

galloping horse, moustache bristling, sabre in hand, as a reminder to all who pass that no one here has betrayed either their roots or their wings.

T H E   R E C I P E S   O F   A U V E R G N E   A N D   L I M O U S I N

●●●●●●●●●●●●●●●●●●●●●●●●●●●●●●●●●

Légumes Secs en Salade 56

Saumon aux Lentilles 79

Foie de Veau à la Moutarde 137

Chevreuil en Ragout 151

Cèpes Sautés 168

Truffade 176

Poires a la Fourme d'Ambert 186

Carottes Vichy 157

BURGUNDY

It is easy to fall in love with Burgundy. From the vantage point of its gentle green slopes, you look down on creamy majestic Charolais cows, Romanesque churches, brilliantly coloured tiled roofs, lazy canals and lively rivers. And in the midst of it, best of all, are the 'salty Burgundians' themselves with sparkling eyes, pink cheeks, accents that leave an 'rrrrr' lingering in the air, and their outrageous appetite for life.

A stream of irresistible energy runs through the region. Burgundy has more abbeys, castles, statues, restaurants, vineyards, freshwater fish, game, and more rivers and canals – 1200 kilometres in all – than any region in France. But even so, in Burgundy such abundance never seems excessive.

Touching the regions of Île de France, and Lyonnais, bordered by the Alps and the Seine, Loire, and Rhône rivers, Burgundy is shaped by its four main cities: Sens in the north, Nevers to the west, Mâcon in the south, and to the east the 'sacred market', Dijon, its capital since the fourteenth century.

For centuries Burgundy has been both the physical and spiritual heart of France. Body and spirit have always walked hand in hand here. The good fortune Burgundy has received from nature has made it a desirable acquisition for many peoples. Over the centuries, Celts, Romans, Greeks, Germans and a multitude of others have inhabited Burgundy as merchants, traders, pilgrims, crusaders and settlers, each contributing to the tumultuous history and also adding something to the personality of this glorious province.

At the centre of the vital network of waterways and roads linking the

BURGUNDY

Auxerre

Saulieu

Dijon

Beaune

Nevers

Loire

Saône

Bresse

Louhans

Mâcon

Switzerland

Mediterranean with northern Europe, Burgundy has been both a cross-roads and a meeting place throughout the ages. Excavations in Solutre show man was here as long ago as twenty-five thousand years and it was in Burgundy, at Alesia, that Caesar defeated the Gauls. By the four-teenth century, Dijon was the capital of the Duchy of Burgundy, Europe's most powerful state and a strong rival to France's royal court. As monks, artisans and farmers cleared forests and built houses, churches and castles they also tended pastures, nurtured vineyards and bred livestock. In doing so, they laid the foundations of Burgundy's cooking and today, the whole province lives under the spell of food.

Burgundy has some of the world's best beef cattle which are reared in Auxois and Charollais, its renowned poultry is bred near Bresse and there are forests full of game and mushrooms – mousserons, girolles, cepes, and morilles. The region abounds with fish in its many rivers and springs and it seems to produce almost everything else, from honey to snails to the tastiest of berries. Patient artisans transmute local ingredients into traditional regional products such as mustard, cheese, gingerbread, and the wonderful liqueur of Cassis that is used in *Sablé aux pommes et au Cassis* (see pp. 200–1).

But, as full of promise as these ingredients and products are, what matters is knowing how to turn them into lusty, full-bodied dishes, and this often means drawing on Burgundy's medieval tradition of mingling the sweet and the salty which also happens to be very much today's taste. There are sumptuous and celebrated stews such as *Boeuf Bourguignon* (see pp. 140–1) and *Coq au Vin* (see pp. 117–19), redolent with mustards, spices, cream, garlic, onions, and wine. But there are also a great variety of simple meals such as 'gougères' to enhance a good wine, fresh dandelion leaves seasoned with warm vinegar and cured ham as in *Pissenlit aux lardons et à la vinaigrette* (see p. 52), fragrant meat pies, mustard and chive omelettes and snail and herb casseroles such as *Escargots à la Bourguignonne* (see p. 108). There are superb fish dishes like *La Pauchouse* (see p. 70), and for dessert, pears cooked in spicy wine such as *Poires, Pruneaux, et Oranges au Vin Rouge et aux Épices* (see p. 192). The much cherished regional dish 'raisiné' is made up of crushed grapes reduced to a pasty syrup in which pears and quinces are turned – a dish that would have made the eyes of the most difficult Duke of Burgundy sparkle with pleasure.

More than just a part of stews and 'meurette' sauces, wine is an equal partner in Burgundy's ongoing love affair with food. Proud as they

are of their renowned Pinot Noirs and Chardonnays, Burgundians see wine not as a privilege of the happy few but as a birthright for all to enjoy together. In a region of boundless energy and appetite, wine should be approached gently, without haste or abrupt excesses. True Burgundians believe wine is best enjoyed from a large glass with a narrow rim so that the air can get into the glass as it is slowly swirled but so the bouquet cannot get out.

Each of us has our own idea of heaven. Some of my friends in Burgundy tell me that theirs would be to have throats in the form of a corkscrew so each swallow of wine, each bite, might be enjoyed longer and better. Following in the footsteps of their illustrious Ducal ancestors, today's Burgundians want both quality and quantity. Here more than anywhere else, happiness, like the ripe fruit on a tree, is there for anyone who is willing to take it.

THE RECIPES OF
BURGUNDY

●●●●●●●●●●●●●●●●●●●●●●●●●●●●●●●●●

PROVENCE

Provence seems to need hardly any introduction. Its purple hills of juniper and lavender, its sleepy villages perched on the hillsides, its honey coloured 'mas' and whispering fountains have been rediscovered many times over. Following on the tracks of the hunters who discovered the region a million years ago, visitors like Cézanne, Van Gogh, Picasso, Dufy, Cole Porter, Colette, Somerset Maugham, and Pagnol have made this among the most celebrated of places.

Provence, bordered by the Mediterranean coast in the south, the Rhône river to the west and the Alps in the east has several quite distinct personalities. To the north there is a secret hinterland where flowers, trees and rocks, heated by the sun, exhale heady fragrances. From here, the River Rhône winds its way south to the coast past lively cities, Roman arenas and aqueducts, and fields of fruit and vegetables. Provence's coastal region stretches from Marseilles' bustling harbour through vineyards and olive groves to the glamorous Riviera with 225 kilometres of coast running from St Tropez to the Italian border. Finally, there is modern Provence with its universities, electronics and pharmaceutical plants, computer and marine-biology research centres, and a highly developed transportation network.

The question about this region today is how much of what has made it unique is still here to discover and enjoy. Can we still blend into an open marketplace and share the fun of a village Festin, a game of Pétanque and a pastis in the shade?

The truth is that much of Provence is every bit as beautiful today as it was when Renoir and Matisse first painted it. It is not, however, a quaint museum. It is a vigorous and lively region moving, as we all are,

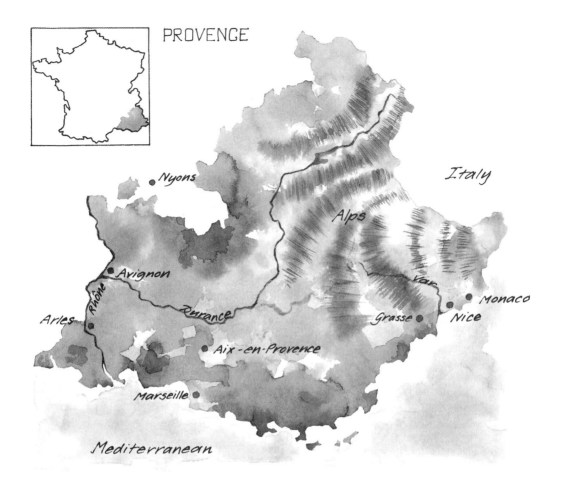

into a new century. So, while the three-hundred-year old olive oil mill near my house in Grasse keeps turning our tiny harvest of olives into the most precious of oil, trucks have replaced donkeys at the mill and a fax and computer keep track of account details.

As Provence grows and changes along with the rest of the world, what remains unchanged and continues to make it irresistible is its extravagant range of colours, architectural forms and dazzling fragrances. As for its two most celebrated assets – the sun and the carefree disposition of the natives – the usual clichés don't always apply.

Provence has more hours of sunlight than any other region in France, and there is no doubt the sun is part of its magic. The motto of Provence is still the words of the cicada's song, *le soleil me fait chanter*, 'the sun makes me sing'. However, Provencaux and Provençales like to sip the sun with infinite precaution as if it were an intoxicating potion, drop by drop. The elaborate game of hide and seek between shade and light is played on many keys in Provence. Shady trees, narrow streets, small windows with wooden shutters, beaded curtains on the doors to screen out the heat, parasols, vine-screened terraces, bamboo beach-parasols and jasmin gazebos, all reflect the ambiguous welcome given the sun.

As for the carefree, good temper of the villagers, it is mingled with an impetuous, curious, demonstrative streak that is often blamed on the Mistral wind blowing fiercely down the Rhône Valley bending giant cypress trees and exciting the temper of those in its path.

In the villages of Provence with their ochre and peach houses and blue and green shutters, beyond the fountain, the church, the ancient trees there is always the strategically place Bar-Tabac. People stroll by, observe one another, sit on a low wall in a shaded square watching the activity of the pizza truck, eyeing the market's goods, in other words, making the most out of every encounter. They kiss, shake hands, exchange jokes, tips and thoughts, and tease each other with bittersweet memories.

With snow-capped Alps only an hour from the coast, grey pebbled rivers, flower-strewn islands, sand and rock beaches, the turquoise sea, rich plains, exotic suspended gardens and oriental villas, the region feels and often looks like paradise on earth. But it is the men and women of Provence who have turned a '*gueuse parfumée*', a poor but fragrant region, into fertile orchards, vegetable farms, and luscious flower gardens thanks to irrigation, railways, lots of imagination and hard work. Everywhere, it is this ever-present heritage, the intricate honey-coloured stone walls, the dainty campaniles, the mossy fountains which best reflect Provence's graceful union of man and nature.

Cookery here is a vital part of daily life. Provençal cuisine is pungent, spirited and built around seasonal produce. The region around Cavaillon and Nice is sometimes referred to as the market garden of France. Everyone here tries to grow a row of green beans, a few tomatoes, a courgette plant, and a few pots of basil and mint. *Ratatouille* (see page 154), *Beignets de Courgettes* (see p. 58), *Salade Niçoise* (see p. 52) and the wide range of vegetable sauces, gratins and soups express this appetite for fresh, inexpensive local products. Near the coast, fish is a cornerstone of the cookery. The most famous regional fish soup is *Bouillabaisse* (see p. 73). *Soupe de Pêcheurs* (see p. 72) is made with the humblest fish

T H E   R E C I P E S   O F   P R O V E N C E

•••••••••••••••••••••••••••••••••••

from the day's catch and enhanced by the fiery red peppers *Rouille Sauce* (see p. 48) while *Bourride* (see p. 68) is a more refined fish soup which uses lean white delicate fish and is enriched with spoonfuls of *Aioli*, the garlic mayonnaise (see p. 48).

Tapenade, Pistou, Anchoïade (see pp. 48–50), *Aïoli, Rouille*, all these potent sauces are also used as dressings for boiled vegetables, grilled meats and fish as well as for dips for *Crudités* (see p. 46), the region's favourite snack. They are also wonderful when simply spread on toasted bread for a snack.

People in Provence turn away from rich, elaborate preparations. They prefer spirited little dishes such as plates of small stuffed vegetables called *Petits Farcis* (see p. 60) or *Rougets Grillée aux Feuilles de Vigne* (see p. 90) that use the anise-scented herb, fennel, to flavour grilled fish. What matters here is not quantity but the intensity of each flavour; olives, saffron, herbs, lemon, garlic, vinegar, capers, bitter almonds and, of course, virgin olive oil are all used to give character and zest to a variety of dishes. Meats especially lamb (see p. 132), poultry, fish and vegetables are all enhanced by the addition of a few herbs and spices and served crisp and fragrant with all their natural juices absorbed.

Like the legendary lizard on the sundial which only counts the sunny hours, people here know that, as in politics, happiness is about reaching for what is possible. They count the world's blessings, they laugh, they turn a meal, a chat, a mindless game into a shared pleasure. They only count the rich hours.

STARTERS

Les Entrées

....

*C*RUDITÉS

Raw vegetables with a selection of sauces

Crudités are a blessing whenever you feel lazy and want to enjoy your own party. A wide assortment of raw vegetables along with a selection of sauces for dipping into, such as *Tapenade, Anchoïade* and *Pistou* encourage relaxed conversation. The sauces can be prepared in advance and kept, covered, in a cool place or the refrigerator, and the vegetables can be arranged on the platter or in the basket, sprinkled with a little cold water, covered with cling film and refrigerated.

Any left-over vegetables can be seasoned with one of the sauces and mixed with a few tablespoons of *Vinaigrette* to make a salad. Alternatively they can be transformed into vegetable soup. All the sauces serve about 4 people.

*V*EGETABLES

Choose a selection from the following list. Quantities are according to the occasion.

radishes with 1 inch (2.5 cm) stem

button mushrooms, trimmed, with part of the stem on

chicory leaves, halved lengthways if wide

cauliflower florets

mange-touts

watercress sprigs

spring onions with 2 inch (5 cm) of their green stems

carrots cut into sticks or whole spring carrots with their green leaves

cucumbers, peeled, seeds removed, cut into sticks

broccoli florets

fennel bulbs, cut into sticks

celery sticks about 3 inches (7.5 cm) long

small green asparagus spears, about 4 inches (10 cm) long

green, red and yellow peppers, cut into sticks

sprigs fresh flat-leaved parsley

sprigs fresh basil

Place the vegetables on a platter or in a basket, and garnish with a few sprigs of parsley and basil.

MAYONNAISE

Mayonnaise is one of the most versatile of sauces, and it is one of the easiest to prepare despite what some people believe. All the ingredients should be at room temperature, a kitchen towel should be placed under the bowl to prevent it from sliding as you beat the sauce, and the oil must be added slowly. If the mayonnaise separates, place a fresh egg yolk in a clean bowl, add a little mustard and start stirring, slowly adding the curdled mixture until the sauce is silky and firm.

1 large egg yolk
1 teaspoon Dijon mustard
4 fl oz (120 ml) olive oil and 4 fl oz (120 ml) groundnut oil or 8 fl oz (250 ml) groundnut oil

about 1¹/₂ teaspoons white or red wine vinegar, to taste
salt and freshly ground black pepper

Beat the egg yolk and mustard with a hand-whisk for 1 minute, then beat in about a quarter of the oil, a drop at a time, until it is incorporated into the sauce. When there is a tablespoon or so of firm mayonnaise you may proceed a little more quickly but always with an attentive eye and a steady hand. When all the oil is absorbed add the vinegar and season.

Variations

Lemon Mayonnaise Omit the vinegar and add about 1¹/₂ teaspoons lemon juice.

Herb Mayonnaise Stir 2 tablespoons chopped mixed fresh herbs into the mayonnaise.

Curry Mayonnaise Stir 2 teaspoons curry powder into the mayonnaise.

VINAIGRETTE

1¹/₂ tablespoons white wine vinegar
6 tablespoons olive oil, vegetable oil or a mixture
1¹/₂ teaspoons Dijon mustard

2 tablespoons finely chopped mixed fresh herbs
1¹/₂ tablespoons finely chopped shallots
salt and freshly ground black pepper

Vigorously stir all the ingredients together in a small bowl, or shake them together in a screw-top jar.

ROUILLE

This fragrant sauce is based on the same principle as Mayonnaise except it is made with a pestle and mortar. If your pestle isn't big enough to take all the oil transfer the garlic, when crushed, to a larger bowl. Keep all the ingredients at room temperature, place the mortar on a cloth and add the oil gradually.

4 garlic cloves
1 large egg yolk
4 fl oz (120 ml) olive oil
4 fl oz (120 ml) groundnut oil

juice 1 lemon
¹/₂ teaspoon saffron threads, crushed
1 teaspoon cayenne pepper
salt and freshly ground black pepper

Crush the garlic cloves in a mortar, then pound them to a paste. Add the egg yolk, stirring and pounding constantly, then gradually stir in oil as you did for the Mayonnaise (see page 47). When the sauce is firm and all the oil incorporated, stir in the lemon juice, saffron, cayenne pepper, salt and pepper; the sauce should then be smooth and quite firm. After 1 hour in the refrigerator it will thicken.

AÏOLI

5 garlic cloves
2 small egg yolks
¹/₂–1 teaspoon Dijon mustard

5 fl oz (150 ml) groundnut oil
5 fl oz (150 ml) olive oil
salt and freshly ground black pepper

Crush the garlic cloves in a mortar, then pound them. Stir in the egg yolks and mustard. When smooth, continue as for making Rouille.

Above: Tree-lined rivers and canals eloquently speak
Burgundy's name.

Previous page: Kayserberg, Alsace. Sloping roofs and long
eaves help to keep the snow at bay in the winter.

PISTOU

I use *Pistou* (in Provence it is called a *pommade* or 'creamy mixture' rather than a sauce) to flavour vegetable soup, fill raw tomatoes and flavour fresh noodles. I spread it on browned lamb chops, hamburgers and crisp toast, and I stir it into warm rice. When there is not enough basil, I use fresh mint or flat-leaved parsley, just like everyone in the Alps used to do. I cannot grow basil in winter so sometimes I freeze *Pistou* for the cold-weather months.

5 cloves garlic, crushed
1 teaspoon salt
2 handfuls basil leaves
4 fl oz (120 ml) olive oil

2 oz (50 g) Gruyère, Parmesan or
pecorino romano cheese, grated
freshly ground black pepper
salt

Crush the garlic and coarse salt in a mortar to make a paste, or use the back of a fork and a small mixing bowl. Pour into a blender or food processor with the basil leaves and olive oil and mix on a high speed. Add the grated cheese, pepper and a little salt if needed and mix for an instant.

Note
If the *Pistou* is too thick, add a peeled, seeded and sieved tomato and a little oil.

TAPENADE

Tapenade is most often made with Nyons olives, or any plump black variety, but plump green olives are occasionally used to make an interesting variation.

The name comes from *tapenado*, Provençal for 'capers' which were used to enhance the olives and cover any faults.

I spread *Tapenade* on baked fish or warm, crisp chicken, I add a spoonful to beef stew, I use it to stuff hard-boiled eggs, tomatoes, cucumbers and sticks of celery. I spread it on boiled chicory or celery hearts, and it gives new life to sliced, cold beef or pork. I also add a handful of stoned olives to *Tapenade* then stir it into rice or fresh noodles. *Tapenade* can be frozen.

——————— *Serves 4–6* ———————

7 oz (200 g) plump black
   olives, stoned
6 anchovy fillets, crushed
2 tablespoons capers
2 cloves garlic, crushed
1 teaspoon fresh thyme

1 tablespoon Dijon mustard
juice 1 lemon
4 fl oz (120 ml) olive oil
freshly ground black pepper
1 tablespoon brandy (optional)

Put all the ingredients in a blender or food processor. Mix at a high speed for 1 second until smooth and soft; if necessary, add a few more drops of oil. Pour into a bowl. Just before serving adjust the seasoning, if necessary.

ANCHOÏADE

Anchoïade is more pungent when made with anchovies that have been kept in brine rather than those packed in oil.

   I like to spread *Anchoïade* on grilled red mullet; I toss it with raw fennel salad, and with thickly sliced hot potatoes, I season warm bean, lentil or chickpea salads with it, but I mostly love it on warm slices of bread.

——————— *Serves 4–6* ———————

20 anchovy fillets packed in brine
   or in oil
5 tablespoons olive oil

1 tablespoon wine vinegar
2 cloves garlic, crushed
salt and freshly ground black pepper

If using anchovies that have been packed in brine, rinse very well to remove excess salt, then pat dry. Place all the ingredients in a blender or food processor then mix at a high speed for 1–2 seconds. Season to taste and transfer to a bowl. Stir well before serving.

Variation

For *Bagna Cauda*, warm *Anchoïade* with 1 teaspoon butter and serve as a dip for raw celery, tiny raw purple artichokes and cardoons.

PROVENCE

FROMAGE DE CHÈVRE À L'HUILE D'OLIVE

Goats' cheese marinated in olive oil

Jenny Fajardo de Livry and her family live practically under the craggy cliffs of Les Baux in Provence. Out of her window are the sounds of gentle bees, the ticking of cicadas and the faint bleating of goats from nearby farms.

Fresh goats' cheese has a lovely mild taste on its own, but Jenny marinades it with a tasty olive oil and pungent flavourings. The longer the cheese is left, the stronger it will taste. If you cannot find small, soft fresh cheeses, cut a round log cheese into slices, each about 1½ inches (4 cm) wide. If this is not possible try using a dry, crumbly goat's cheese – it will do just as nicely.

Serves 4

4 small fresh goats' cheese, or 4 slices
   of a log cheese
salt and freshly ground black pepper
4 sprigs summer savory, or thyme

4–6 tablespoons virgin olive oil
1–2 tablespoons marc, or brandy

Place the cheese on a plate. Season with salt and pepper and scatter the leaves from the herb sprigs evenly over the top of the cheeses. Spoon over the oil and marc, or brandy, and leave for 30 minutes.

Note

If you want the cheese to have a stronger flavour, leave them in a cool place, but not the refrigerator, for 2–3 hours, basting the cheeses with the oil and marc, or brandy, occasionally.

*P*ISSENLIT AUX *L*ARDONS, ET À LA VINAIGRETTE

Warm dandelion, or spinach, and endive salad with bacon

Tossed with a pungent dressing and garnished with crisp croûtons flavoured with garlic and olive oil, this salad makes an invigorating first course or a refreshing accompaniment to a rich main course such as Roast Duck with Spinach Stuffing (see page 124).

———————— *Serves 8* ————————

2 tablespoons vegetable oil
8 oz (225 g) lean bacon or lean salt pork, cut into ¹/₂ inch (1 cm) dice
about 8 handfuls crisp dandelion leaves, or young spinach leaves or endive

4 tablespoons red wine vinegar
2–3 teaspoons Dijon mustard
salt and freshly ground black pepper
4 slices wholemeal or good firm white bread, made into Small Garlic-flavoured Croûtons (see page 85)

Heat the oil in a heavy-bottomed frying-pan, add the bacon or pork and fry until crisp.

Meanwhile, fill a salad bowl with hot water to warm it. Empty and dry the bowl. Tear the dandelion or spinach leaves into pieces and put into the bowl. Pour over the bacon or pork and the warm cooking juices.

Stir the vinegar into the frying-pan, bring to the boil, then stir in the mustard. Pour over the salad. Sprinkle with pepper, and a little salt if needed. Add the Croûtons, toss and serve.

———————— **PROVENCE** ————————

*S*ALADE *N*IÇOISE

Mixed raw vegetable salad with eggs, anchovies, tuna and olives

Give us our daily *Salade Niçoise*! Throughout the summer, whether eating in a gazebo covered with jasmine, on a terrace overlooking the sea or under an olive tree on a wooden table, a *Salade Niçoise* is always a part of a meal in Provence. The fresh, crisp vegetables, pungent flavours and light dressing capture perfectly the spirit of the area.

In Provence, most people try to grow their own row of vegetables and almost every household has some basil growing in a pot on the window sill or balcony. In Provence and along the Riviera all the towns and villages have markets offering piles of vegetables, fresh herbs, and barrels of olives so that from May to October everybody can easily find the ingredients to prepare *Salade Niçoise*. It can be dressed up or dressed down and although everyone has their own favourite recipe, cooked vegetables such as potatoes, green beans and beetroot do not belong in a true *Salade Niçoise*. Neither does raw fish. The only acceptable fish are tuna packed in olive oil and anchovies kept in brine or olive oil. The tradition is to use either anchovies or tuna, but I use them *both*.

———————— *Serves 4* ————————

1 small cucumber

4 firm, fleshy tomatoes, seeds removed, thickly sliced

5 oz (150 g) very young, fresh broad beans (optional)

4 small purple artichokes, quartered (optional)

1 fennel bulb, very thinly sliced

2 small green or red peppers, sliced

4 small spring onions, thinly sliced

4 oz (100 g) radishes with short green stems

2 hard-boiled eggs, peeled and halved lengthways or quartered

6 anchovy fillets, rinsed

1 × 7 oz (200 g) can tuna packed in oil, drained

4 oz (100 g) small black Nice olives, or larger, oil-cured black olives, stoned

salad leaves such as rocket, batavia or lettuce

FOR THE DRESSING

8 tablespoons virgin olive oil

salt and freshly ground black pepper

2 cloves garlic, crushed

10 leaves fresh basil or mint, finely chopped

Peel and slice the cucumber, then place on paper towels for 10 minutes, to drain.

To make the dressing, mix together the oil, salt, pepper, garlic and basil or mint.

Arrange the salad vegetables, eggs, anchovy fillets, tuna and olives attractively in a wide, shallow dish, then surround with salad leaves. Pour over the dressing and take the dish to the table without stirring it. Just before serving toss lightly.

*C*ÉLERI *R*ÉMOULADE

Celeriac salad

Raw, shredded celeriac tossed with a pungent mustard-flavoured mayonnaise is a popular dish in bistros, where it is often served as a first course with a bowl of grated carrots seasoned with lemon juice, a dish of diced boiled beetroot seasoned with parsley, and a bundle of pink radishes. It is also served at buffets and taken on picnics.

Celeriac discolours soon after it has been grated, so add the dressing at once. Cream and Vinaigrette dressing are both good with celeriac.

——————— *Serves 4* ———————

1 celeriac bulb	*5 fl oz (150 ml) vegetable oil, or a mixture of vegetable and olive oil*
FOR THE DRESSING	*approximately 1 tablespoon white wine*
1 egg yolk	*vinegar or lemon juice*
2 tablespoons Dijon mustard	*salt*

To make the dressing, beat the egg yolk and mustard together for 1 minute, then beat in about a quarter of the oil, a drop at a time, until all the oil is incorporated into the sauce. When there is about 1 tablespoon of firm sauce, the oil can be added a little more quickly. Add vinegar or lemon juice and salt to taste.

Using a heavy, sharp knife, quarter the celeriac, then peel it. Grate the celeriac into a serving bowl, add the dressing and stir to mix. Cover and chill lightly.

Variations

Cream dressing Mix together the juice of 1 lemon and 2 tablespoons Dijon mustard, then stir in 10 fl oz (300 ml) whipping or double cream. Add salt and whisk lightly, if liked.

Vinaigrette dressing Stir 2 tablespoons finely chopped fresh chives, tarragon or chervil into Vinaigrette (see page 47).

POIREAUX VINAIGRETTE

Warm leek salad

Every serious bistro in France boasts a *Poireaux Vinaigrette*. Leeks are sometimes called the poor man's asparagus, and certainly when prepared in this way, they can be classed as a 'Great Simple Dish'. Choose firm, white leeks and only use the white part.

———————— *Serves 4* ————————

8 slim leeks, each about 5 inches (12.5 cm) long
2 teaspoons Dijon mustard
salt and freshly ground black pepper
1 tablespoon white or red wine vinegar
2 hard-boiled eggs, peeled

4 fl oz (120 ml) virgin olive oil
2 tablespoons coarsely chopped fresh parsley

TO SERVE
warm, toasted wholemeal bread

Slice the leeks in half lengthways and rinse under cold running water. Tie the leeks with string into 4 bundles and cook in salted boiling water for about 10 minutes, until just tender.

Meanwhile, in a bowl, stir together the mustard, salt, pepper and vinegar. Cut the eggs into halves lengthways then scoop the yolks into the bowl. Mash them together with a fork then slowly mix in all but 1 tablespoon of the oil until the dressing is smooth.

Drain the leeks well then remove the strings. Lay the leeks on several layers of paper towels, cover with more paper towels and leave for a few minutes to absorb the excess moisture. Transfer the leeks while still warm to a heated serving dish and pour over the egg yolk dressing. Finely chop the egg whites and sprinkle over the leeks with the parsley and the remaining oil. Serve warm or at room temperature with a basket of warm, toasted wholemeal bread.

LÉGUMES SECS EN SALADE

Warm chickpea, or haricot bean, salad

One of France's main culinary skills has always been the knack of transforming ordinary ingredients into something special. In Limousin, warm *mojettes*, small, white haricot beans, are served with pungent dressings. I saw an entire family involved in the preparation of the main ingredient of this dish! Each family member had a role: the growing, picking and drying of the beans was done by the son; the separating of the stalks from the pods was undertaken by the grandparents; and finally the game of jumping on the piles of dry, discarded stems was practised with equal fervour by both the family dog and the small children.

A handful of rocket, dandelion leaves or corn salad adds a refreshing texture and flavour to the dish. Warm salads such as this can be served as a first course or as accompaniment to plainly cooked meat.

Serves 4

12 oz (350 g) chickpeas or haricot beans, soaked overnight then drained and rinsed
1 carrot, halved
1 onion, halved, studded with 1 clove
1 bay leaf
1 sprig fresh thyme

TO GARNISH
chopped, fresh, flat-leaved parsley, chives, or tarragon

FOR THE DRESSING
1 tablespoon finely chopped fresh parsley
2 spring onions, finely chopped
3 tablespoons olive oil
1 tablespoon red wine vinegar
1 tablespoon Dijon mustard
1 teaspoon finely chopped fresh chives or tarragon
$1/2$ teaspoon freshly grated nutmeg
salt and freshly ground black pepper

Place the chickpeas or beans in a saucepan with the carrot, onion, bay leaf and thyme. Add plenty of cold water and boil for 10 minutes. Cover and simmer for $1-1^1/2$ hours, until tender.

Meanwhile, mix together all the dressing ingredients. Drain the chickpeas or beans and discard the vegetables and herbs. Put the warm chickpeas or beans in a warm china or earthenware serving bowl and pour over the dressing. Toss gently and sprinkle with parsley, chives or tarragon. Serve warm.

Variation

In Provence, chickpea, lentil and white bean salads are dressed whilst warm but served at room temperature; a dressing flavoured with 3 garlic cloves and 3 crushed anchovy fillets is often used.

—— **NORTH–WEST FRANCE** ——

*H*ARENGS *S*AURS
Marinated cured herring fillets

A true bistro staple that is a particular speciality of Boulogne. Just a look at the big brown or white dishes of *harengs saurs* on the table will tell you whether you are in a serious place or not.

This is one of the easiest dishes to prepare at home, and it will keep covered in the refrigerator for at least one week. *Harengs saur* are salted and smoked whole; for convenience and availability kipper fillets can be substituted for them.

———— *Serves 4* ————

8 harengs saur *or kipper fillets, each about 5 inches (13 cm) long*
1 onion, sliced
1 carrot, sliced
2 bay leaves
1 sprig thyme
1 lemon, sliced
10 black peppercorns

about 8–10 fl oz (300 ml) mixed olive oil and groundnut oil
fresh flat-leafed parsley leaves

TO SERVE
good country bread and unsalted butter, or warm sliced potatoes seasoned with oil, vinegar, parsley or chives, and salt

Place the kipper fillets in the bottom of an attractive, round or rectangular, white china or brown earthenware dish. Cover with the onion, carrot, bay leaves, thyme, lemon and peppercorns. Pour over sufficient oil to cover generously. Cover the dish with foil or cling film and leave in the refrigerator for at least 2 days, turning the fillets over twice during that time. Sprinkle over the parsley and serve at room temperature with the bread or potatoes.

Variation

Add 1 or 2 crushed garlic cloves an hour before serving.

BEIGNETS DE COURGETTES
Courgette fritters

I was brought up nibbling crisp fritters and have eaten them as *hors d'oeuvres*, vegetable accompaniments, desserts and snacks. I have had fritters made with flaked salt cod, anchovies, whitebait, aubergines, courgettes, artichokes, acacia and courgette blossom. Piping hot, crunchy outside and soft inside, I still cannot dream of a greater treat.

I enjoyed the following recipe in Grasse. Annick Pellissier and her mother, Yvonne, prepared them almost with their eyes closed, resembling well-schooled dancers as they moved around the kitchen with quick, confident gestures, light feet and skilful hands. Meanwhile, Annick's son laid the table under the lemon and pepper trees, and her husband and I gathered wild salad leaves from the garden.

——————— *Serves 4* ———————

7 or 8 courgettes, coarsely grated
salt
15 fresh mint leaves
vegetable oil, for frying

FOR THE BATTER
6 oz (175 g) plain flour
2 large eggs, separated
7 fl oz (200 ml) beer
1 teaspoon olive oil
freshly ground black pepper

For the batter, put the flour into a large bowl, make a well in the centre, add the egg yolks, beer, and olive oil, then gradually stir the flour into the liquids to make a smooth batter. Cover and leave in a cool place for 1 hour.

Place the courgettes in a sieve, sprinkle with salt then place a plate on the courgettes and a weight on the plate. Leave for 1 hour. Rinse the courgettes under cold water then dry with paper towels. Stir the courgettes and mint leaves into the batter and season with pepper.

Whisk the egg whites until stiff but not dry then, using a tablespoon, gently fold into the batter.

Heat the oil in a frying-pan, then add tablespoonfuls of the courgette mixture. Cook for 3–4 minutes on each side until golden brown. Using a fish slice, transfer the fritters to paper towels to drain. Keep warm while frying the remaining mixture. Serve hot.

PETITES COURGETTES ET TOMATES FARCIES

Stuffed courgettes and tomatoes

I was served these delicious, light stuffed vegetables by Annick Pellissier as I sat in the sun with her family overlooking the fragrant, herb-covered hills of Grasse. As long courgettes are more readily available than round Nice ones, I have made the recipe using them.

——— *Serves 4–6* ———

3½ tablespoons fresh breadcrumbs	8 oz (225 g) lean minced beef
2 tablespoons milk	2 small eggs, beaten
4 courgettes	4 tablespoons crème fraîche
5 tomatoes	6 tablespoons chopped fresh basil
3½ tablespoons olive oil	salt and freshly ground black pepper
1 onion, finely chopped	1 oz (25 g) Gruyère cheese, grated

Pre-heat the oven to gas mark 5, 375°F (190°C). Butter a baking dish.

Leave 1½ tablespoons of the breadcrumbs to soak in the milk. Cut the courgettes in half lengthways and then, using a teaspoon, carefully scoop out the seeds and flesh from the centres, and chop finely. Cut a small slice from the tops of 4 tomatoes and carefully scoop out and discard the seeds from the tomatoes. Place them upside down to drain. Skin the remaining tomato, discard the seeds and chop the flesh.

Heat 1½ tablespoons oil in a frying-pan, add the onion and cook over a moderate heat, stirring occasionally, for about 5 minutes, until softened. Stir in the chopped courgette flesh and the chopped tomato and cook for a further 2–3 minutes. Remove from the heat and stir in the beef, eggs, crème fraîche, basil, salt and pepper. Squeeze the soaked breadcrumbs dry and stir into the pan. Divide the mixture between the courgettes and tomatoes.

Place the filled vegetables in the baking dish. Sprinkle the remaining breadcrumbs, cheese and olive oil over the vegetables. Bake for about 25 minutes until the courgettes are just tender and the topping is brown. Serve hot, warm or cold.

PETITS FARCIS
Stuffed vegetables

In Provence, onions, courgettes, aubergines, tomatoes, peppers and even dainty courgette blossoms are filled with many different ingredients, but usually the stuffing is made from what is at hand or in the garden. There may be basil, thyme, a slice of ham, a piece of chicken, grated cheese, garlic, a bit of this, a pinch of that – all are welcome as long as the stuffing is light and fragrant and complements the vegetables. *Petits Farcis* are nicknamed 'bishop's mouthfuls' because they are always small, but although their size is small, the variety and quantity of vegetables served is always generous, and there should be at least four *Petits Farcis* per person. *Petits Farcis* can be eaten surrounded by sprigs of basil or parsley and piping hot, lukewarm or cold; and they may be served at picnics, buffets, lunches or dinners.

Serves 4–6

4 tablespoons olive oil
2 small aubergines
2 medium-sized tomatoes
2 small green or red peppers, top and stem cut off, seeds and central stem discarded
2 whole onions
2 medium-sized courgettes
1 onion, chopped
2 oz (50 g) lean streaky bacon
1 tomato, skinned, seeds removed, chopped

8 oz (225 g) beef, lamb, ham or chicken, or lean streaky bacon finely chopped
4 oz (100 g) cooked rice
8 tablespoons finely chopped fresh flat-leaved parsley
1 tablespoon fresh thyme
2 cloves garlic, crushed
salt and freshly ground black pepper
2 eggs, lightly beaten
2 oz (50 g) Parmesan or Gruyère cheese, grated
2 oz (50 g) fresh breadcrumbs

Pre-heat the oven to gas mark 4, 350°F (180°C). Oil a baking sheet.

Brush the aubergines with $1/2$ tablespoon olive oil and place on the baking sheet. Bake for about 15 minutes until soft. Leave until cool enough to handle then cut into halves lengthways and scoop the flesh from the aubergines into a large bowl. Leave a $1/2$ inch (1 cm) shell and take care not to pierce the skin.

Cut the tomatoes in half lengthways, sprinkle with salt and leave them upside-down on paper towels for 10 minutes. Gently squeeze out the excess juice and scoop out the pulp. Place the pulp in the bowl.

Meanwhile, bring a large saucepan of salted water to the boil, add the peppers and boil for 5 minutes then add the whole onions and boil for about 5–7 minutes. Add the courgettes and continue to boil for a further 5 minutes. Drain all the vegetables and leave until cool enough to handle.

Cut the onions in half crossways, then remove the centres leaving about 2 layers of skin. Put the centres into the bowl with the aubergine flesh and tomato pulp.

Cut the courgettes in half lengthways and, using a teaspoon, scoop the flesh into the bowl. Using kitchen scissors, chop the vegetables which are in the bowl.

Pre-heat the oven to gas mark 5, 375°F (190°C). Brush 1 or 2 baking sheets with oil and place all the vegetable shells on them.

Heat 1 tablespoon olive oil in a frying-pan and add the chopped onion and bacon. Cook gently for 4–5 minutes, until tender. Stir in the flesh from the vegetables, the chopped tomato then the beef, lamb, ham or streaky bacon or chicken, rice, parsley, thyme, garlic, salt and pepper. Cook, stirring occasionally, for 3–4 minutes then remove from the heat and stir in the eggs. Divide between the vegetable shells then sprinkle the cheese and breadcrumbs over the tops. Trickle over the remaining olive oil and bake for about 20 minutes. Serve hot, warm or cold.

Variation

In Nice, chopped Swiss chard, a few anchovies, and grated Parmesan cheese are often added.

PISSALADIÈRE

Onion and anchovy tart

This is Nice's special onion tart. It is sold in markets, bakeries, *traiteurs*, and charcuteries. It is eaten in restaurants, on picnics, in the streets, at home, by the seashore. As always in France, every cook has their very own definite way of making the best *Pissaladière*, including me. Some love a thick soft crust, some a light crisp one, some have a thin layer of onions, some cover the base with a thick blanket of onion purée, some add garlic and thyme and some prefer anchovy fillets to the traditional puréed anchovies (called *pissalat*, hence the name of the tart).

————— *Serves 4* —————

FOR THE DOUGH
8 oz (225 g) strong white flour
1 teaspoon salt
2 teaspoons easy-blend yeast
onion liquid (see method)
lukewarm water (see method)
4 teaspoons olive oil

FOR THE FILLING
2 tablespoons olive oil
2¹/₂ lb (1.25 g) medium-sized yellow
  onions, thinly sliced
2 garlic cloves, crushed

1 bay leaf
3 sprigs fresh thyme
salt and freshly ground black pepper

FOR THE GARNISH
1¹/₂ tablespoons fresh thyme
15 anchovy fillets, halved lengthways
approximately 16 whole, small black
  Nice olives, or 12 large, oil-cured
  black olives, stoned and halved
1 teaspoon olive oil
freshly ground black pepper
basil leaves (optional)

For the filling, heat the olive oil in a large frying-pan, add the onions, garlic, bay leaf, thyme, salt and pepper (the salt will draw water from the onions, preventing them drying) and cook gently, stirring occasionally with a wooden spoon, for about 1¹/₂ hours, until the onions are very soft. Remove from the heat, discard the bay leaf and thyme then squeeze the onions gently to one side of the pan with a slotted spoon, draining off the liquid into a measuring jug. Make up to 5 fl oz (150 ml) with the water.

Sift the flour and salt into a large bowl. Stir in the yeast, form a well in the centre, and slowly pour in the onion liquid and 1 teaspoon olive oil, stirring constantly to make a smooth dough. Beat well until the dough comes away from the sides of the bowl, then transfer to a lightly-floured surface and knead well by stretching the dough away from you using the heel of one hand to push the dough from the centre outwards. Pull it back with the fingers, slap it on the work surface and repeat the process, turning the dough slightly with each movement. Continue for about 15 minutes until the dough is soft, smooth and elastic. Add a little more olive oil if it is not supple enough. Form the dough into a ball, place in an oiled bowl and turn it over. Cover with a damp cloth and leave in a warm place until doubled in volume, about 1¼–1½ hours.

Pre-heat the oven to gas mark 7, 425°F (220°C). Oil a 9 × 13 inch (23 × 33 cm) Swiss-roll tin or a 10–11 inch (25–28 cm) round, flat tin.

Turn the dough on to a lightly floured surface, and punch it down. Roll out the dough using a lightly floured rolling pin, to a rectangle approximately 9 × 13 inches (23 × 33 cm) or 10–11 inch (25–28 cm) round. Lightly fold one half of the dough back over the rolling pin then carefully transfer to the baking tin. Press the dough into the corners and slightly up the sides.

Taste the onion purée to check that the seasoning is correct and then spoon it evenly over the dough. Sprinkle over the thyme. Arrange the anchovy fillets on top in a lattice pattern or like the spokes of a wheel if using a round tin, and place olives in the spaces. Sprinkle the top with olive oil and freshly ground pepper.

Bake for 25–35 minutes, depending on the thickness of the base, until the dough has shrunk slightly from the sides of the tin and is golden and crisp. Remove from the oven and serve warm garnished with basil. If the *Pissaladière* is cooked in advance, sprinkle it with olive oil and reheat for 15–20 minutes in a low oven.

Note

To use dried yeast, measure 4 tablespoons of the onion/water mixture into a small bowl, and stir in ½ teaspoon caster sugar. Sprinkle 1½ teaspoons dried yeast over the surface, stir once and leave until there is a good head of froth, about 10–15 minutes. Pour into the well in the flour with the remaining onion/water mixture.

To use fresh yeast, pour the 5 fl oz (150 ml) of onion/water mixture into a small bowl, crumble over ½ oz (15 g) fresh yeast then blend in using a teaspoon. Add to the flour as in the recipe.

*T*ARTE *F*LAMÉE

Alsace pizza

This is one of Alsace's most popular dishes. It is baked in special wood ovens at a high temperature for a short time so that the pastry is very crisp but the onions and bacon on top are barely cooked. In a pretty inn, the *Bürestubel* in Pfulgriesheim, just outside Strasbourg, I saw a cook bake 370 *Tarte Flamées* in one evening. They were served piping hot on a long-handled wooden rectangular baker's shovel.

As I tried to reproduce *Tarte Flamée* at home I found that a very hot oven really was important, and that the onions and bacon had to be finely cut and not cooked at all before being put on the dough to be baked. A mixture of soft curd cheese and soured cream makes a good substitute for the fresh cheese used at the *Bürestubel*.

The problem is that once you can make a good *Tarte Flamée* one is never enough, and two, three or four always seem to be needed because it is so easy for everyone to become addicted to them.

— *For 1* tarte *serving 4 as a starter* —

10 oz (275 g) strong plain flour
1 teaspoon salt
1½ teaspoons instant dried yeast
4 fl oz (120 ml) warm water
1 egg, beaten
1 teaspoon vegetable oil

FOR THE TOPPING
4 oz (100 g) soft curd cheese
5 fl oz (150 ml) soured cream
salt and freshly ground black pepper
1 tablespoon groundnut oil
4 oz (100 g) streaky bacon, cut into ¼ inch (5 ml) wide strips
1 onion, cut into slivers

Sift the flour and salt into a large bowl and stir in the yeast. Form a well in the centre and pour in the water, egg and oil. Using a wooden spoon, gradually draw the dry ingredients into the liquids then beat well until the dough comes away from the bowl. Turn on to a lightly floured surface and knead for 10–15 minutes until the dough is elastic and smooth. Form

Opposite: PISSALADIÈRE (*see page 62*) In Nice, Pissaladière is simply a bed of onions with an olive and a slice of Anchovy on top – it has no crust at all.

into a ball and place in an oiled bowl, cover with a clean, damp cloth, and leave to rise in a warm place for 1 hour.

Pre-heat the oven to gas mark 8, 450°F (230°C). Butter a large baking tray.

Turn the dough on to a lightly floured work surface, punch it down then knead briefly before rolling it out as thinly as possible to a rectangle approximately 13 × 9 inches (33 × 23 cm). Fold the dough back over the rolling pin and carefully lift it on to the tin. Use your fingers to ease it into shape.

Mix together the cheese, soured cream, salt, pepper and groundnut oil for the topping and spread on the dough. Sprinkle with the bacon and onions. Bake for 20 minutes until the edges are crisp and slightly charred. Serve hot and eat, rolled or folded with your fingers.

Note

To use dried yeast, measure 2 tablespoons boiling water into a small bowl, add 2 tablespoons cold water and stir in ½ teaspoon caster sugar. Sprinkle 1½ teaspoons dried yeast over the surface, stir once and leave until there is a good head of froth, about 10–15 minutes. Pour into the well in the flour with the egg yolk and oil and only 2 fl oz (50 ml) more water.

To use fresh yeast, heat the 4 fl oz (120 ml) water in the recipe until it is lukewarm, pour into a small bowl, crumble over ½ oz (15 g) fresh yeast, then blend in using a teaspoon. Add to the flour with the egg and oil.

Opposite: MARMITE DIEPPOISE (*see page 74*).

PAN BAGNAT

Moist salad sandwich

Pan Bagnat, which means 'bathed, or moist, bread' in Provençal, is a flavourful and healthy sandwich that has never ceased to be popular along the Riviera. It is eaten as a light meal or snack in market-places, on the beach or on picnics by everyone.

Traditionally local bakers made a big round loaf for *Pan Bagnat*, but today smaller rolls are used, as well as lengths of *baguettes*, small *pains ronds* or, as a last resort, a hamburger bun from the supermarket.

Serves 4

4 round rolls, or an approximately 10 inch (25 cm) long piece of baguette

4 garlic cloves, one halved the others crushed

1 tablespoon white wine vinegar

5 tablespoons virgin olive oil

salt and freshly ground black pepper

4 tomatoes, seeds removed, sliced

1 small cucumber, peeled and sliced

8 small radishes, sliced

2 small green peppers, seeds removed, sliced

4 spring onions with a little green stem, halved lengthways, or 1 onion, sliced

10 fresh basil leaves

3 oz (75 g) small, fresh broad beans (optional)

2 hard-boiled eggs, peeled and sliced

8 anchovy fillets packed in oil, drained and quartered

1 × 7 oz (200 g) can tuna, drained and shredded (optional)

16 black or purple olives, stoned

8 large lettuce leaves

Cut each roll, or the length of *baguette*, in half. Remove and discard a little of the dough from the centre of each piece. Rub the cut surfaces of the bread with a clove of garlic then sprinkle with half of the vinegar and olive oil, and salt and pepper. Pile all the remaining ingredients on one half of each roll or the *baguette*. Sprinkle with the remaining oil and vinegar and season with a little pepper. Cover with the tops of the rolls or the *baguette* and press down very firmly. Wrap in lettuce leaves or aluminium foil and place in the refrigerator for at least 1 hour so all the flavours mingle into the bread, which should become very moist. Traditionally, a weight is placed on the roll or bread to make sure it is 'bathed' properly, but this is not compulsory.

F ISH

Les Poissons

*B*OURRIDE

White fish soup enriched with Aïoli

This rich creamy fish soup is prepared with a variety of white fish, such as monkfish, John Dory, bass, whiting and bream. The ritual is spectacular and the dish glorious.

Some people line a shallow serving dish with thick slices of bread, then pile the pieces of cooked fish on them and finally pour the rest of the soup over. Sometimes the *Aïoli*-thickened-broth is served with crisp, garlicky croûtons as a first course, the fish is coated with the rest of the *Aïoli* and served with steamed potatoes as a second course. Many chefs add a few spoonfuls of double cream to the hot broth to make it truly unctuous. I find this much too rich, but it is definitely worth trying.

In Languedoc, carrots, leeks, celery, Swiss chard and tomatoes are chopped and slowly cooked with pieces of monkfish, then *Aïoli*, diluted with the cooking juices is poured in to make a dish that is more like a stew than a soup.

———— *Serves 8* ————

2 lb (1 kg) monkfish
2 lb (1 kg) sea bass
2 lb (1 kg) bream or whiting
double quantity Aïoli *(see page 48)*
16 slices baguette, prepared as Garlic-
flavoured Croûtons (see page 70)

FOR THE BROTH
3 pints (1.75 litres) water
10 fl oz (300 ml) dry white wine

1 leek, white part only, sliced
1 carrot, sliced
1 onion, sliced
thinly pared rind 1 orange
3 sprigs thyme or 2 teaspoons dried
thyme
2 teaspoons fennel seeds or aniseeds
3 bay leaves
salt and freshly ground black pepper
3 egg yolks

Fillet all the fish and remove the skins; be sure to also remove the fine membrane that covers the monkfish. Reserve the fish bones, heads and skins. Cut the fillets into 1 inch (2.5 cm) pieces.

For the broth, pour the water and wine into a large saucepan, add the fish bones, heads and skin, the leek, carrot, onion, orange rind, thyme, fennel seeds or aniseeds, bay leaves, salt and pepper, bring to the boil, remove the scum that rises to the surface, then simmer for 20 minutes.

Add the pieces of fish to the hot broth, lower the heat and simmer gently for 10 minutes. Using a slotted spoon, remove the fish to a warm, shallow dish. Cover and keep warm.

Pour the broth through a sieve into a saucepan, pushing the bones, vegetables and herbs with a spoon against the sieve. Discard the contents of the sieve. Boil the broth hard for about 3 minutes then keep it warm over a low heat.

Stir the egg yolks into about two-thirds of the *Aïoli*. Gradually stir a ladleful of hot broth into the *Aïoli*, making sure each addition is incorporated before adding the next. Heat the broth to just below simmering point, then slowly pour in the *Aïoli* mixture, stirring constantly. Heat gently, stirring until lightly thickened. Do not allow to boil. Check and correct the seasoning. Pour over the fish and serve with the Garlic Croûtons and the remaining *Aïoli*.

Note

The egg whites that are left can be used to make *Oeufs à la Neige* (see page 188) or *Tuiles* (see page 205).

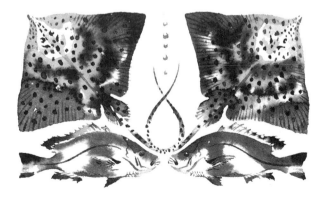

LA PAUCHOUSE

Burgundian fish stew

The best *Pauchouse* I ever ate was prepared in Verdun-sur-le-Doubs. The occasion was not quite in the same league as the banquet which Philippe the Good, Duke of Burgundy, served in 1454 to a few chosen friends, including an emperor and a pope, in order to seal their friendship. In comparison, our gathering was more like Renoir's *Fête Champêtre*, but it had the typical lusty, generous sparkling Burgundy atmosphere.

All around us there were fields of yellow rape, creamy Charolais cattle, tall walnut trees, rivers and canals, and barges. I had joined Monsieur and Madame Bonnot, their daughter, Claude Siegnist, their grandchildren and their friends for a memorable day during which Claude, a Beaune wine *negociant*, and I were introduced into the *Confrèrie de la Pauchoux*. This is a select group of gourmets dedicated to promoting this wonderful Burgundian fish stew. Among much laughter we pledged allegiance to *La Pauchouse* and the formal ceremony was completed by drinking from the traditional silver goblet proferred by our 'brothers', resplendent in their red and yellow robes.

Pauchouse is a medieval dish. The name, which can also be spelt *pouchouse*, *pôchouse* and *pochouse*, is derived from *poche*, the bag in which a fisherman puts his catch. The freshwater fish, such as carp, eel, perch, pike, tench and trout that are abundant in the region, and the local dry white wine are the essence of this dish, but each restaurant and each family has its own tricks to personalise its *Pauchouse*. Most will follow the tradition, though, of using two white fish, such as perch and pike, and two richer ones, such as trout and eel.

——————— *Serves 8* ———————

2 tablespoons groundnut oil	1 pint (600 ml) dry white wine,
2¹/₂ oz (70 g) butter	preferably Burgundy
5 garlic cloves, crushed	2 pints (1.2 litres) fish stock
2 onions, sliced	2 tablespoons flour
2 bay leaves	1 tablespoon brandy (optional)
1 sprig fresh thyme	2 fl oz (50 ml) double cream
10 black peppercorns	4–6 slices good, firm bread, made into
4¹/₂ lb (2 kg) mixed freshwater fish,	Small Garlic-flavoured Croûtons
cut into 2 inch (5 cm) pieces	(see page 85)
salt	

Heat the oil and 1 oz (25 g) butter in a heavy-bottomed saucepan, add the garlic, onions, bay leaves, thyme and peppercorns and cook for about 4 minutes, stirring occasionally. Add the fish, sprinkle with salt and stir gently. Pour in the wine and stock, bring just to the boil then lower the heat and cook gently for 5 minutes, stirring from time to time. Using a slotted spoon transfer the fish to a warm bowl, cover and keep warm.

Blend the flour with the remaining butter to make a *beurre manié*, then gradually whisk into the broth and boil until very lightly thickened. Add the brandy, if using, and boil for a further 2–3 minutes. Stir in the cream, taste and add salt if necessary.

Place the Croûtons in a warm, shallow serving dish, place the fish on top and strain over the broth.

Variation
Red wine may be used instead of white wine, and diced streaky bacon, button onions and mushrooms added.

SOUPE DE PÊCHEURS

Provence-style fish soup

In Provence most fishermen's wives sell their husband's catch every morning in Cannes' market, Forville, Marseille's harbour or under the arcades of St Tropez. They are used to selling the best fish.

The fish which cannot be sold is given to their imaginative talents to turn into family treats. But the 'make something with nothing' principle has always been at the core of French regional home cookery and it is well known that fish soup is generally prepared from almost nothing. Of course if a crab is added, so much the better.

A *Soupe de Pêcheurs* can be one of the most inexpensive of fish soups, and may not contain any actual pieces of fish at all, but the rich broth, the fiery *Rouille* (see page 47) sauce and the crisp Croûtons (see page 85) can be enough to make a heady and delicious soup. It helps if you have a fishmonger who will save fish heads and bones when asked.

Serves 8

5 lb (2.25 kg) mixed white fish such as halibut, cod and monkfish
2 tablespoons olive oil
1¹/₂ tablespoons fresh thyme
salt
2 teaspoons saffron threads
2 tablespoons fennel seeds

FOR THE BROTH
2¹/₂ tablespoons olive oil
2 tablespoons groundnut oil
4 large onions, chopped
2 large leeks, white part only, chopped
6 tomatoes, chopped
6 cloves garlic, crushed
few sprigs fresh parsley
2 lb (1 kg) fish heads and bones, if available

bouquet garni of 1 sprig fresh parsley, 1 sprig fresh thyme and 1 bay leaf
few sprigs fresh fennel or about 2 teaspoons fennel seeds
2 inch (5 cm) piece orange rind, dried in a low oven for 15 minutes
8 sprigs fresh thyme
salt and freshly ground black pepper
2¹/₂ pints (1.5 litres) water
15 fl oz (450 ml) dry white wine
1 tablespoon Pernod (optional)

TO SERVE
Rouille (see page 48)
16 slices baguette, prepared as Garlic-flavoured Croûtons (see page 70)
grated Gruyère or Parmesan cheese

Clean and fillet the fish and cut into 2 × 2 inch (5 × 5 cm) pieces. Reserve the heads, trimmings and bones. Place the pieces of fish in a large bowl, add the olive oil, thyme, salt, saffron and fennel. Toss, cover and leave in a cool place or the refrigerator, for a few hours.

Meanwhile, make the broth. Heat 1$^1/_2$ tablespoons olive oil and a little groundnut oil in a large frying-pan. Add the onions and sauté for about 8 minutes until golden. Add the leeks then the tomatoes, garlic and parsley and cook for 2–3 minutes. Pour into a large saucepan.

Add a little more groundnut oil to the frying-pan and sauté the fish bones, heads and trimmings for a few minutes on all sides. Add the bouquet garni, fennel sprigs or seeds, the orange rind, thyme and salt. Cook for 5 minutes then pour into the saucepan and add the water and wine. Bring to the boil, skim the froth from the surface then cover and simmer for 30–60 minutes.

Add a little fish broth to the *Rouille* and pour into a bowl. Pour the remaining fish broth through a sieve, pressing down on the fish bones and vegetables with a wooden spoon. Discard the contents of the sieve. Taste and add salt and pepper, if necessary.

Heat the broth until it comes to the boil, add the pieces of fish, lower the heat so the liquid barely simmers and cook for 10 minutes. Add the remaining oil and the Pernod, if using. Pour into a large, warm, soup tureen and take to the table with the Croûtons and the cheese.

Pour a ladle or two of soup into each warm soup plate or bowl. Top some of the croûtons with *Rouille* and cheese and float on the surface of the soup. The Croûtons should remain partially crisp as the soup is started. Leave the remaining *Rouille* and bread on the table.

Variation

Bouillabaisse is the most glorious *Soupe de Pêcheurs*. It is made from a variety of different types of white and red fish, such as red mullet, red gurnard, John Dory, monkfish, bream and conger eel. But the most important fish, according to many people, is *rascass*, scorpion fish. This is rarely available away from the Mediterranean, which is why it is often said that it is impossible to make a genuine *Bouillabaisse* anywhere except along the southern French coast. *Bouillabaisse* is really a fisherman's dish, so the fish should either be left whole or cut into pieces, not skinned and filleted. However, I think an adequate *Bouillabaisse* can be made by adding sliced potatoes to a *Soupe de Pêcheurs* – simmer them in the sieved broth for 15–20 minutes before cooking the fish.

MARMITE DIEPPOISE

Creamy mixed fish and seafood flavoured with curry

This hearty soup of fish, shellfish, and vegetables flavoured with curry powder represents the very soul of Normandy. The spices that were first taken to the region by merchant ships returning from the Orient centuries ago beautifully enhance the flavours of local ingredients.

Marmite Dieppoise is a sumptuous dish and it is both easy to make and to serve; the broth can be prepared ahead of time and kept in the refrigerator for even greater convenience. I prefer to serve the guests myself so I can make sure everyone has all the different types of fish.

With *Crudités* (see page 46) as a starter, and a bowl of Fruit Compote (see page 191) for dessert you will have a memorable meal.

--------- *Serves 8* ---------

1³/₄ pints (1 litre)/1³/₄ lb (750 g–1 kg)
   mussels
4 oz (100 g) butter
8 leeks, washed, trimmed, split
   and sliced
5 stalks celery, sliced
2 onions, chopped
1¹/₄ pints (750 ml) dry white wine
salt and freshly ground black pepper
1 carrot, sliced
2 sprigs parsley
2 bay leaves
8 black peppercorns
1¹/₂ lb (750 g) fish bones and fish heads
1³/₄ pints (1 litre) water

8–10 × 4 inch (10 cm) pieces cod and
   either halibut or haddock
8–10 small fillets of sole or plaice
8–10 Dublin Bay prawns
8–10 scallops, shelled (see page 107)
juice 1 lemon
10 fl oz (300 ml) double cream
1–2 teaspoons curry powder
¹/₂–1 teaspoon cayenne pepper

TO SERVE
2 tablespoons finely chopped chervil
   or parsley
4 slices good, firm bread, made into
   Small Croûtons (see page 85)

Leave the mussels to soak for 2–3 hours in a sink or bucket of cold salty water to remove any sand or grit.

Heat 2 oz (50 g) butter in a heavy-bottomed frying-pan. Add the leeks, celery and 1 onion. Cook over a low heat for 4–5 minutes, stirring occasionally, until softened. Tip into a food processor or a blender and mix to a purée. Transfer to a bowl and reserve.

Drain the mussels and scrub the shells with a hard brush. Cut off the beards. Place the mussels in a large saucepan, add half the wine, and half the remaining onion, salt and pepper. Cover and cook over a high heat for 5 minutes, tossing occasionally, until the mussels open; discard any that remain closed. Drain. Pass the liquid through a sieve lined with muslin and then reserve. Remove the mussels from their shells. Place 8–10 shells and all the mussels in a bowl. Discard the other shells.

Heat the remaining butter in a saucepan. Add the remaining onion, the carrot, parsley, bay leaves and peppercorns and cook for 5 minutes. Add the fish bones and fish heads. Pour in the remaining wine and the water, bring to the boil, skim the froth from the surface then simmer for 20 minutes. Pour through a sieve into a larger saucepan, pressing down hard on the fish bones and vegetables, forcing the vegetables through the sieve with a wooden spoon. Add the strained mussel liquid and simmer for a few minutes.

Sprinkle the cod and either halibut or haddock with salt and add to the hot broth. Simmer gently for about 4 minutes, then add the sole or plaice fillets and Dublin Bay prawns, and cook for 3 minutes. Add the scallops and cook for a further 2 minutes. Using a slotted spoon transfer the fish, prawns and scallops to a warm tureen. Add the mussels and mussel shells, sprinkle over the lemon juice, cover and keep warm.

Stir the puréed leeks and celery into the fish broth and boil until reduced to about 2³/₄ pints (1.6 litres). Stir in the cream and add curry powder, cayenne pepper and salt and pepper to taste; the broth should be highly flavoured.

Pour the very hot broth into the tureen and take to the table with warm plates, a bowl of chopped herbs and the Croûtons.

Place a piece of fish, a fish fillet, a Dublin Bay prawn, a scallop, some mussels and a mussel shell on each plate. Spoon a ladleful of soup on top, sprinkle with a little chopped chervil or parsley and add a few Croûtons.

POISSON AU COURT BOUILLON
Poached fish

A court bouillon is the aromatic liquid that is traditionally used for poaching whole, large fish, although it can be used for most fish and even cuts of both fresh and frozen fish such as steaks, cutlets and fillets. There are three kinds of court bouillon, each of which is ideal for a specific purpose (see recipes).

Poaching keeps the fish flesh moist and helps retain the flavour, nutrients and texture. The heads and tails of a whole fish are left on, and as the skin is normally removed before the fish is served, there is no need to remove the scales. Instead of gutting the fish in the usual way by slitting the belly, pull the entrails through one of the gills. Hold the fish's mouth under a cold running tap until the water flowing from the rear vent runs clear. Dry the fish carefully then place on a rack that will fit inside a fish kettle or large, deep roasting tin or similar baking dish. If you do not have a suitable rack, wrap the fish in a piece of muslin or cheesecloth that is large enough for its ends to hang over the sides of the cooking pan. Lower the fish into the fish kettle, tin or dish and cover with the appropriate court bouillon, but do not drown it; large fish should be covered in cold court bouillon, but for small pieces the court bouillon should be warm. Heat to about 160°F (70°C), just below simmering point, and cook for 8–10 minutes for every 1 inch (2.5 cm) of thickness, starting from when the liquid reaches the correct temperature. Using the rack or cloth, remove the fish from the court bouillon. Carefully remove the skin and scrape out the bones lying along the back of the fish. Using two long spatulas, or fish slices, transfer the fish to a large plate.

Whether served warm or cold, the fish can be simply seasoned with lemon juice and perhaps a drizzle of good olive oil. For a more luxurious cold dish, serve with plain, Herb or Curry Mayonnaise, *Aïoli*, *Tapenade*, or *Rouille* (see pages 47–49). If the fish is to be eaten warm, serve with *Beurre Blanc* (see page 81), or warm *Anchoïade* (see page 50).

Steamed or boiled new potatoes, cauliflower, artichoke hearts or asparagus, a vegetable *timbale* such as Spinach (see page 65) or a vegetable purée (see pages 158–161), can accompany warm poached fish whereas cherry tomatoes, lemon wedges, sprigs of parsley, capers, olives, watercress and halved hard-boiled egg go well with it when it is cold.

COURT BOUILLON WITH VINEGAR

Use for fresh-water fish such as pike, trout and carp.

——— *Makes 1³/₄ pints (1 litre)* ———

6 fl oz (175 ml) red wine vinegar
1¹/₂ pints (900 ml) water
1 carrot, chopped
1 small onion, chopped
4 sprigs parsley

1 sprig thyme
¹/₂ bay leaf
salt
4 black peppercorns

Place all the ingredients, except the peppercorns, in a large saucepan, bring to the boil, then simmer for about 20 minutes. Add the peppercorns, cover the pan and remove from the heat. Leave to cool, then pour through a sieve lined with muslin or cheesecloth in to a large bowl.

Court Bouillon with White Wine

Use for whole large fish such as salmon, halibut, tuna and cod. Follow the recipe and method for Court Bouillon with Vinegar using white wine instead of the vinegar.

Court Bouillon with Milk

This should be used to poach very delicate fish, such as sole as its lightness enables the fine flavour of the fish to stand out.

——— *Makes 2 pints (1.2 litres)* ———

10 fl oz (300 ml) milk
1¹/₂ pints (900 ml) water
1 carrot, chopped
1 onion, chopped
4 sprigs parsley

1 sprig thyme
¹/₂ bay leaf
salt
4 black peppercorns

Follow the method for Court Bouillon with Vinegar.

*T*RUITE AU *B*LEU

Poached trout

Those who are lucky enough to have access to a trout stream or live near a trout farm can enjoy this recipe as really fresh fish, preferably those that are live, are essential. But why *au bleu*? Why 'blue trout?' Because if it is handled delicately and neither washed nor dried, the natural coating of slime remains on the fish's skin and the trout develops a bluish tinge when it is cooked. It will also curve whereas a not-so-fresh trout will remain stiff.

─────────── *Serves 4* ───────────

4 whole trout, each weighing
  8 oz (225 g)
7 fl oz (200 ml) white wine vinegar
4 pints (2.25 litres) water
1 carrot, chopped
1 onion, sliced
salt and freshly ground black pepper

TO GARNISH
parsley sprigs

TO SERVE
warm melted butter
lemon juice
finely chopped parsley

If the fish are alive, give a sharp blow to their heads. Carefully pull out the intestines through the gills. Run cold water through the fish from the mouth, taking care not to disturb the slime on the skin, if it is still present. Sprinkle a little vinegar over the fish.

Select a large saucepan, deep frying-pan, or large flameproof dish or baking dish in which you can place the whole trout without bending them. Add the water, remaining vinegar, carrot, onion and salt and pepper, and bring to the boil. Lower the heat so the liquid is just on simmering point, add the fish and poach for 5–7 minutes, until the flesh feels slightly springy to the touch. Remove the fish from the broth and place on paper towels to drain. Transfer to a warm serving plate and garnish with parsley sprigs. Serve with warm melted butter, flavoured with lemon juice and chopped parsley.

Variation

Truite au bleu is also delicious when eaten cold with Lemon Mayonnaise (see page 47).

SAUMON AUX LENTILLES
Salmon with lentils

The lovely Art Deco *Hôtel Radio* perches on a hill in Chamalières over-looking the sombre city of Clermont-Ferrand. The chef-patron, Michel Mioche's much-emulated recipe is the marriage of two Auvergnat in-gredients; salmon from the Allier river and the famous tiny green Le Puy lentils. Pink peppercorns add piquancy to this dish.

If you can't find Le Puy lentils at speciality delicatessens, the larger, flat, dull greenish-brown variety are a good substitute.

——— *Serves 6* ———

14 oz (400 g) tiny green Puy lentils,
  or brown lentils
1 onion, halved
2 cloves garlic
1 bay leaf
1 sprig thyme
3 shallots, finely chopped
³/₄ oz (20 g) butter

4 tablespoons double cream
salt and freshly ground black pepper
2 tablespoons olive oil
6 pieces salmon fillet, each weighing
  about 5 oz (150 g)
1 tablespoon chopped fresh chervil
  or dill
1 teaspoon pink peppercorns.

Rinse the lentils in cold water then place in a saucepan with the onion, garlic, bay leaf and thyme. Cover with cold water, cover the pan with a lid or foil and bring to the boil. Simmer for 25 minutes–1 hour, depend-ing on the quality and freshness of the lentils, until they are tender but not too soft. Drain well and discard the onion, garlic and herbs.

Sauté the shallots in the butter for 3–4 minutes. Add the lentils and cream, season with salt and pepper to taste, cover and keep warm over a very low heat, shaking the pan occasionally.

Heat the oil in a frying-pan. Season the salmon with salt and pepper and cook for about 5 minutes, depending on thickness, so the underside is lightly cooked and the top barely warm. Serve the salmon on the lentils and sprinkle over fresh herbs and pink peppercorns.

Variation
Michel Mioche cuts each piece of fish into strips, then curves the strips round each other to make a flower shape.

SAUMON AU BEURRE BLANC

Poached salmon with white butter sauce

Beurre Blanc remains one of the most celebrated sauces in France at a time when many French sauces have fallen out of fashion. According to the local legend it was invented, albeit by accident, by a Madame Clémence in the 1890s just south of the Loire estuary. *Beurre Blanc* became a speciality of *guinguettes*, the lively little restaurants along the Loire where good, inexpensive food, local Muscadet wine and energetic dancing were all to be found. Farmers, wine-makers and families who worked all week in the busy city of Nantes and who needed fresh air, would meet in the *guinguettes* to enjoy piles of frogs' legs, eels, snails and the exquisite sauce which complemented delicate river fish such as pike and *zander* (pike-perch). Nowadays *Beurre Blanc* is served with a great variety of dishes: poached or grilled seafish and shellfish as well as freshwater fish, poached eggs, asparagus, beans and almost any other steamed or boiled vegetable.

    Beurre Blanc is a simple emulsion of hot, reduced, shallot-flavoured, white wine vinegar or the local wines Muscadet and Gros Plant which have high acidities, and cold butter. It is not a difficult sauce to master providing the liquid is hot, the butter is cold, it is added gradually and is thoroughly whisked. Most people add a spoonful of whipping cream at the last moment to help prevent the sauce turning oily and enable it to be kept a little longer before being served.

Opposite: SAUMON AUX LENTILLES (*see page 79*).

—————— *Serves 4* ——————

4 pieces of fillet of salmon, each
  weighing 5 oz (150 g)
approximately 15 fl oz (450 ml) Court
  Bouillon with Vinegar
  (see page 77)

FOR THE BEURRE BLANC
3 tablespoons white wine vinegar

3 tablespoons Muscadet, Gros Plant or
  other dry white wine
8 tablespoons finely chopped shallot
8 oz (225 g) lightly-salted
  butter, diced
salt and freshly ground black pepper
1 tablespoon whipping cream or Court
  Bouillon with Vinegar (see page
  77), (optional)

Lay the salmon in a single layer in a frying-pan, pour over sufficient *Court Bouillon* to cover and bring just to simmering point. Cover with a piece of buttered greaseproof paper, butter-side down, and poach gently for 5–6 minutes. Using a fish slice, transfer the salmon to a warm plate, cover and keep warm.

Meanwhile, make the *Beurre Blanc*. Bring the vinegar and wine to the boil in a small, thick-bottomed, stainless steel saucepan. Add the shallot and simmer very gently, uncovered, until soft and the liquid reduced to 1 tablespoon. Add one piece of butter at a time, whisking vigorously after each addition. Do not allow the mixture to boil. The sauce will thicken and become white and frothy. Off the heat, add salt and pepper to taste, and the cream if liked. Pour into a warm sauceboat and serve with the salmon.

Variation

Monsieur Jean-François Hatet, chef at the *Auberge Nantais*, St.-Julien-de-Concelles, sautéed the salmon in butter for 3–4 minutes each side.

Note

The sauce can be kept warm over hot water or over the pilot light of a gas stove for about 30 minutes. If it does separate, pour a little sauce into a very cold bowl, beat firmly until it is smooth again, then gradually add the rest of the sauce.

Opposite: BAR AU VIN ROUGE (*see page 82*).

BAR AU VIN ROUGE

Sea bass with red wine sauce

Burgundy boasts an abundance of good wine, good fish, good poultry, serious home-cooks and ambitious chefs. But although the half-timbered houses, ivory coloured mansions and varnished roofs speak of permanence and evoke continuity, cookery in Burgundy is a living art and as such is constantly evolving. In fact, during the last few years it has done many, perhaps *too* many, acrobatic performances. Fortunately, although the French tend to be thrilled by innovation and love to be surprised and fashionable, they also know that home cooking based on local products remains the true barometer of a good chef. So even Michelin three-star chefs in very sophisticated restaurants appreciate the value of the regional cuisine.

The following recipe resulted from a delicious meal we enjoyed in Saulieu at the restaurant *Côte d'Or*. Monsieur Bernard Loiseau, who for over ten years has been both inventive and controversial and praised and criticised, uses the best Burgundian ingredients, works with local farmers, fishermen and cheese makers and blends traditional methods with modern techniques. His *Bar au Vin Rouge* is an inspired combination of tastes and textures and gains much of its character from the skilful partnership of a red wine with a fish. The fish is cooked on one side only so that it remains crisp and is not overcooked, the sauce is thickened with a carrot purée to balance the wine reduction and the shallots provide a complementary flavour.

———————— *Serves 4* ————————

4¹/₂ oz (120 g) unsalted butter
12 oz (350 g) shallots, thinly sliced
salt and freshly ground black pepper
2 tablespoons sugar
8 oz (225 g) carrots, sliced

1¹/₂ pints (900 ml) soft, fruity red
* wine, such as Gamay*
1 tablespoon groundnut oil
4 fillets sea bass
2 teaspoons plain flour

Heat 1¹/₂ oz (40 g) butter in the frying-pan, add the shallots, sprinkle with salt and cook over a low heat for about 25 minutes, stirring occasionally. Off the heat, tilt the frying-pan to one side then, using a slotted spoon draw the shallots to the other side of the pan so the liquid drains away then transfer the shallots to a saucepan. Sprinkle over the sugar, cover and cook over a low heat for a further 25–30 minutes until the mixture turns into a purée.

Meanwhile, cook the carrots in boiling, salted water until tender. Drain well, then purée. Boil the wine until reduced to 5 fl oz (150 ml). Stir in the carrot purée then lower the heat and gradually whisk in 2 oz (50 g) of the butter. Remove from the heat, season with salt and pepper, cover and keep warm over a very low heat.

Heat the remaining butter and the oil in a wide frying-pan over a high heat. Season the fish, sprinkle flour lightly over the skin then place in the pan, skin-side down, and cook for about 4–5 minutes. Do not turn the fish, but put a lid on the pan, and cook over a very low heat about 2 minutes. Remove the pan from the heat.

Pour a quarter of the wine sauce on each plate, add a quarter of the shallots then place a piece of fish, skin-side up, in the centre of each plate.

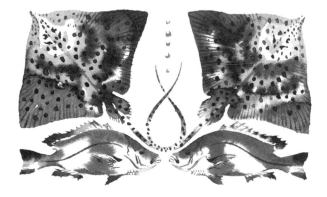

SOLE MEUNIÈRE
Sole fried in butter with lemon and parsley

Familiarity does not always bring contempt. *Sole Meunière* is a staple in French cookery, yet when a fresh, tender sole is carefully browned, coated with fresh parsley, lemon and good butter, its perfection still pleases. After all, it is the most sympathetic way of cooking this light fish. *Sole Meunière* is served all over France but in Normandy where fresh sole and good butter abound, it is at its very best.

Why *meunière*, miller's style? Probably because of the flour that is used to protect the delicate skin of the sole as it cooks, and to make it crisp as it browns. The coating of flour should only be light, though, and the butter for frying needs to be hot. It is for this reason that the butter is clarified, so removing the fine particles that burn at high temperatures and which spoil the appearance and flavour of this delicate dish.

Diced, peeled cucumber sautéed in butter, or grapes are fitting accompaniments.

—————— *Serves 4* ——————

6 oz (175 g) unsalted butter, diced
3 tablespoons flour
salt and freshly ground black pepper
4 sole, about 12 oz (350 g) each, heads
    and dark skin removed and filleted
juice 2 lemons
2 tablespoons finely chopped fresh
    flat-leaved parsley

FOR GARNISH
parsley sprigs
lemon wedges

TO SERVE
steamed tiny new potatoes

First, you must clarify 4 oz (100 g) butter. To do this, heat it gently in a small saucepan until it foams. Carefully skim the foam from the surface and pour the clear butter slowly through muslin wrung out in very hot water into a small bowl, leaving the milky sediment behind.

Season the flour with salt and pepper and place on a plate. Dip the fish in the seasoned flour to coat lightly and evenly.

Heat the clarified butter in a large frying-pan until it sizzles. Add 1 or 2 fish – it is vital that they are not crowded – and cook over a moderate heat for about 4–5 minutes on each side until crisp but not brown. Shake the pan from time to time and turn the fish with a fish slice.

Using the fish slice, transfer the fish to a warm plate. Keep warm. Fry the remaining fish in the same way.

Pour the cooking juices from the pan and wipe the pan with paper towels. Add the butter that has not been clarified to the pan and heat until it foams and turns light golden brown. Add the lemon juice and parsley then pour immediately over the fish. Garnish with parsley sprigs, add lemon wedges, and serve with steamed potatoes.

Variation

The same method is suitable for small whole fish such as trout, flounder, small whiting and small bass, or for fish fillets (if the fish are large the outside would become dry before the inside was cooked).

CROÛTONS

Pre-heat the oven to gas mark 6, 400°F (200°C). Brush one side of each slice of *baguette* with olive oil or spread with butter, then place on a baking sheet and bake for 2 minutes. Turn the slices over, turn the oven off and bake the bread for a further 3 minutes, until crisp.

Small Croûtons
Cut slices of good, firm bread about ½–¾ inch (1–2 cm) thick. Brush with oil or spread with butter, then bake in the same way as Croûtons, until just becoming crisp then cut the bread into cubes.

Triangular Croûtons
Cut slices of good, firm bread about ½ inch (1 cm) thick. Continue as for Small Croûtons, but cut each slice into 6 or 8 triangles.

Garlic-flavoured Croûtons
Rub the baked bread with a cut garlic clove. Then cut into cubes if making Small Croûtons.

Herb Croûtons
Sprinkle finely chopped fresh herbs over the baked bread.

LOTTE À L'ARMORICAINE

Monkfish with tomato, herb, garlic and wine sauce

The following recipe is adapted from a sumptuous meal I ate in Audierne, on the very tip of Brittany. In this most mystical of places contrasts exist side by side – granite and fig trees, mimosa and a grey ocean. The inhabitants are used to challenges being the descendants of valiant fishermen and bold pirates. Monsieur Adolf Bosser, the chef-patron of the *Le Goyen* restaurant, is the living embodiment of those virtues and so is his cuisine.

The origin of this sauce is a matter of debate – is it *Armoricaine* from *Armorique*, the old name for Brittany, or *Americaine* after a restaurateur in Paris who had spent some time in America and adapted a recipe from his native Languedoc, which seems plausible because of the tomatoes, garlic and herbs used in the recipe? According to Monsieur Bosser, it is most definitely *Armoricaine*. It is so obviously a Brittany sauce! Where else could a sauce with such energy and flavour and so perfect for local fish and shellfish originate? Only a Breton could have created such a rich sauce. As few home cooks have shellfish shells to hand for making the sauce, I have adopted Monsieur Bosser's recipe, but the spirit prevails.

Lobster is the traditional main ingredient but it is so very expensive that monkfish (the so-called poor man's lobster because the two fish have similar textures) is considered a perfect substitute. Other firm-fleshed fish such as cod will also be enhanced by the spirited sauce.

I suggest serving buttered rice or tiny boiled potatoes, and steamed vegetables with *Lotte à l'Armoricaine*.

———— *Serves 6* ————

2 skinned monkfish tails, each
   weighing about 1¹/₂ lb (750 g)
salt and freshly ground black pepper
3 tablespoons olive oil
1¹/₂ oz (40 g) butter
1 small leek, chopped
1 onion, chopped
2 small shallots
1 clove garlic, crushed
5 tomatoes, chopped

1–2 tablespoons tomato purée
2 sprigs thyme
1 sprig tarragon
¹/₂ bay leaf
15 fl oz (450 ml) dry white wine
2 tablespoons brandy
cayenne pepper
1 teaspoon sugar (optional)

TO GARNISH
chopped fresh parsley and tarragon

Remove and discard the fine membrane covering the monkfish tails, fillet each tail then slice into approximately 2 inch (5 cm) pieces on the diagonal. Season lightly.

Heat the oil and $^1/_2$ oz (15 g) butter in a deep, heavy-bottomed frying-pan or saucepan and sauté the fish for a few minutes, turning from time to time, until brown on all sides. Transfer the fish to a warm plate. Cover with foil.

Add the leek, onions, shallots and garlic to the pan and cook very slowly for 5 minutes, until soft. Stir in the tomatoes, tomato purée, thyme, tarragon, bay leaf, wine and brandy. Bring to the boil then simmer the sauce for 20 minutes.

Strain the sauce through a sieve then pour back into the pan. Add the fish and cook gently for 8–10 minutes. Add a little cayenne pepper and check the seasoning. Add a little sugar, if necessary, to balance the acidity of the tomatoes. Away from the heat, stir in the remaining butter. Serve garnished with parsley and tarragon.

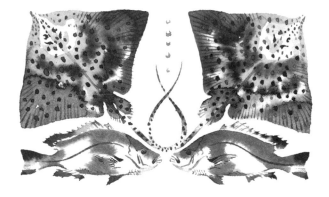

*D*AURADE AU *F*OUR

Baked bream with fennel, lemon and herbs

An uncomplicated dish, but the ingredients must be fresh.

——— *Serves 4* ———

4 tablespoons olive oil

3 onions, thinly sliced

1 fennel bulb, trimmed, thinly sliced
into rounds

about 10 sprigs fresh parsley

2 bay leaves

salt and freshly ground black pepper

2³/₄ lb (1.25 kg) bream, halibut or
bass, filleted

4 tomatoes, seeds removed, sliced

4 teaspoons fennel seeds or aniseeds

1 lemon, sliced

5 tablespoons dry white wine

3 or 4 large Iceberg coarse lettuce
leaves

juice of 1 lemon

Pre-heat the oven to gas mark 4, 350°F (180°C).

Heat 2 tablespoons olive oil in a frying pan, add the onions and fennel and cook over a moderate heat, stirring occasionally, for about 5 minutes until beginning to soften.

Place half of the onions and fennel, the parsley, and 1 bay leaf in a baking dish. Sprinkle with a little salt and pepper. Lay half of the fish on top, skin side down, sprinkle with salt, pepper and olive oil. Place the remaining fish on top, skin side up. Cover with the tomatoes, remaining onions, fennel and bay leaf, the fennel seeds or aniseeds and the lemon slices. Pour over the wine and a little olive oil.

Lay a few lettuce leaves loosely on top and bake for about 25 minutes until the flesh is milky when tested with the tip of a knife. Discard the lettuce leaves. Using 2 fish slices, carefully transfer the fish to a warm serving dish. Sprinkle with the lemon juice and a little pepper, then trickle over the remaining olive oil and serve immediately.

VENDÉE

SARDINES EN BROCHETTES

Sardine and pepper brochettes

I discovered this simple dish on the charming island of Noirmoutier, in the Atlantic ocean just off the Vendée coast. Noirmoutier is a holiday resort which resembles a Greek island, with its stark windmills and whitewashed, blue-shuttered cottages. The sardines were prepared using the local fragrant sea salt, newly harvested and smelling faintly of violets. They were served with the renowned Noirmoutier Charlotte potatoes.

From Brittany to Provence there are endless ways of using sardines – raw with lemon and oil, marinated in lemon juice, grilled, stuffed and fried. In this dish they are treated very simply. Dipping them in sea salt adds flavour and makes them easier to fold onto the skewers.

Serves 1

4 sardines, each weighing about
   4 oz (100 g)
about 3 oz (75 g) coarse sea salt
$^{1}/_{2}$ teaspoon dried thyme
1/2 red pepper, cut into $1^{1}/_{2}$ inch
   (4 cm) pieces

$^{1}/_{2}$ green pepper, cut into $1^{1}/_{2}$ inch
   (4 cm) pieces
$^{1}/_{4}$ onion, separated into layers, cut into
   $1^{1}/_{2}$ inch (4 cm) pieces
$1^{1}/_{2}$ tablespoons olive oil
freshly ground black pepper

Pre-heat the grill.

Working from tail to head and using a knife, scrape the scales from the sardines. Slit along the underside of each fish then remove the intestines. Cut off the heads. Open out each fish and place, skin-side up, on a board. With a thumb, press lightly along the centre of the back of one fish, then turn the fish over and lift away the backbone. Leave the boned fish in coarse sea salt for 30 seconds. Remove from the salt and carefully brush off all the excess. Sprinkle over a little thyme and pepper.

Brush the peppers and onion with olive oil and sprinkle with sea salt and pepper. Skewer sardines, red pepper and green pepper and onion alternately along a skewer until all the ingredients have been used. Grill for 5–8 minutes, turning a few times.

ROUGETS GRILLÉS AUX FEUILLES DE VIGNE

Barbecued red mullet

On Lulu Peyraud's estate near Bandol we witnessed the old saying 'the family who cooks together enjoys life together' at work as we followed the cheerful group from the vineyard, to the kitchen, to the long table under the tall shady, trees for a long and chatty meal.

Lulu owns the beautiful *Domaine Tempier*, where she has a lovely, informal herb garden by her kitchen door. Her husband and sons make their olive oil and wines which fill a large, cool cellar nearby.

When Lulu and I returned from Bandol market with our baskets filled with fish, I realised all the family was involved in the preparation of our meal. Monsieur Peyraud, his son and daughter-in-law had already laid wood and vine twigs in the huge fireplace in the centre of the kitchen, and a bundle of savory and a neat pile of vine leaves were waiting on the table. Now Lulu was going to barbecue the red mullet we had bought – while I sipped a glass of wine and nibbled a few olives.

If the fish are fresh, the fire very hot and the herbs fragrant, Barbecued Red Mullet is one of the simplest and most delicious of dishes. The fish quickly cooks to become crisp outside, moist inside and fragrant all over.

Red mullet should not be gutted or scaled as emptying the fish removes part of the flavour, and the scales protect the flesh against becoming dry during the cooking.

Serve with rice flavoured with bay leaves and olive oil, and sliced courgettes or fennel sautéed in olive oil.

———— *Serves 4* ————

4 whole red mullet, with heads and
    tails on, each weighing 1 lb (450 g)
4 sprigs fresh fennel, or 3–4
    tablespoons fennel seeds
juice 1 lemon
salt and freshly ground black pepper
4 teaspoons fresh savory, if available
2 tablespoons olive oil

8 vine leaves, or thick lettuce leaves
large pinch dried herbs

FOR THE GARNISH
sprigs of fresh flat-leaved parsley
    or watercress
slices of lemon

Pre-heat the barbecue.

Rub the outside of the fish lightly with a paper towel. Place a sprig of fennel or some fennel seeds on each fish and sprinkle lemon juice, salt and pepper, savory, if available, and a little olive oil over the skin then wrap each fish in a vine leaf or thick lettuce leaf to help keep the fish moist; as the fish cooks the leaves crumble away. Place the fish in a double-sided barbecue fish grill.

When the barbecue is almost white-hot sprinkle a large pinch of dried herbs over the wood or charcoal and place the fish grill over it. Cook the fish for about 8 minutes on one side, turn them over and cook the other side for about 10–15 minutes, depending on the thickness of the fish, until the flesh flakes easily and becomes opaque. Brush away the dry vine or lettuce leaves, place the fish on a warm serving plate and garnish with watercress or parsley, and sliced lemons.

Variation

Mash a small knob of softened butter with 1 anchovy fillet and a little fresh pepper and place on top of each fish as it is about to be served.

NOTE

The fish can also be cooked on a grill rack beneath a hot grill.

SAINT PIERRE À L'OSEILLE

John Dory with sorrel

According to the legend, the two black spots which are on the sides of a John Dory are the prints of Saint Peter's fingers, hence the fish's French name – St Pierre. It is a delicate sea fish which closely resembles sole in texture and flavour.

In France, sorrel is eaten both in omelettes and soups as well as being used to enhance white meats and fish. In this recipe sorrel is mixed with flour and cream to soften its acidity and make it a good complement to the delicate flavour and texture of John Dory.

——————— *Serves 4* ———————

$1^{1}/_{2}$ oz (40 g) unsalted butter
8 oz (225 g) sorrel, about 4 handfuls,
    stems removed, shredded
    with scissors
1 teaspoon flour

1 tablespoon double cream
2 egg yolks
salt and freshly ground black pepper
$2^{3}/_{4}$ lb (1.25 kg) John Dory, filleted

Pre-heat the oven to gas mark 5, 375°F (190°C). Butter a shallow ovenproof dish.

Heat half of the butter in a saucepan. Add the sorrel and stir with a wooden spoon over a moderately high heat until the leaves have wilted and any liquid evaporated. In a small bowl, stir together the flour, cream and egg yolks. Stir into the sorrel. Cook gently, stirring, for about 3 minutes until lightly thickened; do not allow to boil. Add salt and pepper to taste.

Place half of the sorrel mixture in the dish then lay the fish fillets on top. Sprinkle with salt and pepper and pour over the remaining sorrel mixture. Dot with the remaining butter and bake for 20 minutes until the fish flakes easily when tested with the point of a knife.

*L*A MORUE
Dried salt cod

Dried salt cod is available in many different ways today. Throughout France, it is sold in grocers and supermarkets sometimes as a whole fish, fins and tail included and as hard as wood, sometimes as fillets, it is sometimes packed in a little wooden box, and sometimes wrapped in plastic and frozen. In Nice, dried salt cod is often sold soaking in a pan of running water so that it is ready to be cooked at once.

For centuries, dried salt cod has been served on Fridays, during Lent and on Christmas days because the Papacy decreed these to be meatless days. Dried salt cod is therefore often referred to as 'the lean days' beef', although recently it has also become fashionable and is served on any day of the week.

Dried salt cod is mainly eaten along the Mediterranean, but in other areas such as Brittany, Auvergne and Burgundy, it can be found in a variety of local dishes.

Dried salt cod must be soaked for about 24 hours in several changes of water before being cooked. Place the soaked fish on a heatproof plate or an upturned small, heatproof dish in the saucepan so the fish does not touch the bottom of the pan, and to allow the salt to drop easily. Cover with cold water and bring to the boil. Lower the heat, poach gently for 3–5 minutes depending on size, then remove the pan from the heat and leave the fish to cool in the water.

Dried salt cod can become a true ally in the kitchen because it can be used to make a great many different light and pungent dishes. It may be either served in 2 × 2 inch (5 × 5 cm) pieces, shredded or puréed. It may be flavoured with cream, garlic, oil and lemon, red or white wine, melted butter, Vinaigrette (see page 47) or béchamel sauce. It can be added to potatoes, onions, tomatoes, spinach, leeks, anchovies or peppers, or it may be included in a spinach gratin or *Bouillabaisse de morue* or turned into fritters, croquettes or a salad.

Always choose thick fillets, preferably those that have come from the centre of the fish, and allow about 4 oz (100 g) dry weight, per person.

BRANDADE

Salt cod and potato purée

Dried salt cod has been a staple of French Mediterranean cookery for centuries. It was taken to Provence and Languedoc by Norwegian and other traders from northern waters who went to the Mediterranean to buy olive oil, vegetables and fruits. It is still very popular and is prepared in innumerable ways.

The process which transforms a hard, dry, grey piece of fish into *Brandade*, an ivory, fluffy mousse, is not a complicated one. It used to require endurance and a steady hand as the ingredients were pounded in a mortar and then stirred over a low heat but today, with the help of a blender or a food processor *Brandade* is child's play. And whereas traditional *Brandade* required a great amount of olive oil, the recipe I use now contains less oil but more milk and potatoes so is lighter and less rich. When it is served as a white pyramid, sprinkled with black olives and surrounded by crisp Croûtons it makes a splendid, fragrant dish. Any *Brandade* that is left over makes a delicious filling for an omelette, formed into croquettes, or used as a base for poached eggs.

A large bowl of crisp salad leaves such as endive, chicory or rocket seasoned with *Vinaigrette* (see page 47) is a good companion for *Brandade*.

―――――― *Serves 6* ――――――

1½ lb (750 g) dried salt cod
2 bay leaves
1 onion, studded with 1 clove
1 lb (450 g) potatoes, unpeeled
10 fl oz (300 ml) milk
8 fl oz (250 ml) olive oil
3 cloves garlic, crushed
2 teaspoons grated nutmeg
juice 1 lemon or 1 orange

freshly ground white pepper
2 tablespoons Niçoise or black Greek
*   olives, halved if large, stoned*
3 slices good, firm bread prepared as
*   Triangular Croûtons (see page 85),*
*   or 6 slices baguette, prepared as*
*   Croûtons (see page 85)*
1 tablespoon chopped fresh parsley

Place the dried salt cod in a large saucepan or basin and cover with cold water. Soak for at least 24 hours, changing the water 5 or 6 times.

Drain the dried salt cod then place on an upturned heatproof plate or small dish in an enamelled or stainless steel saucepan and cover with cold water. Add the bay leaves and onion and bring slowly to the boil. Lower the heat, poach for 3 minutes, then turn off the heat and leave the cod to cool in the water. Drain well, remove the skin and any bones and flake the flesh with a fork.

Cook the potatoes in boiling water until soft. Drain well, leave to cool then peel and press through a sieve.

Warm the milk and all except $1^1/_2$ tablespoons of the oil in separate saucepans. Place a few pieces of cod in a blender or food processor and mix briefly. Add the garlic and more flaked cod, and continue processing, alternately pouring in milk and oil, and adding cod until you have a smooth ivory purée. Transfer to a bowl and gradually beat in the potato. Add nutmeg, lemon or orange juice and pepper.

Transfer to a warm shallow dish. Sprinkle over the remaining olive oil, stir and mound into a dome. Arrange the olives in the centre of the dome. Dip a tip of Triangular Croûtons, or edge of large ones into the *Brandade*, then into chopped parsley and place round the edge of the dish.

Note
Brandade can be prepared in advance. Warm through gently and beat in 2 tablespoons warm milk or cream.

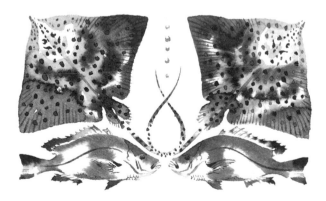

Suppions Farcis
Stuffed squid

Squid are lean, and reasonable in price so I serve them in many guises, but on very hot summer days the following recipe is light and refreshing. I use spinach for the stuffing as it is widely available but a sorrel and Swiss chard mixture (use the green part of the Swiss chard and keep the stalks for another dish) can be used in place of the spinach. As a variation two chopped, hard-boiled eggs and 2 teaspoons fresh breadcrumbs can be added with the spinach.

———— *Serves 4* ————

2 lb (1 kg) small whole squid
2 tablespoons olive oil
3 oz (75 g) spring onions, white part
 only, finely chopped
3 garlic cloves, crushed

6–7 oz (175–200 g) cooked, drained
 spinach, or Swiss chard
salt and freshly ground black pepper
2 tablespoons chopped fresh flat-leaved
 parsley, or basil

Pre-heat the oven to gas mark 4, 350°F (180°C).

Rinse the squid then, holding the head just below the eyes, gently pull it away from the body pouch. Discard the soft innards that come away with it. Pull out and discard the fine, flexible, transparent quill that is attached to the inside of the pouch. Cut the head from the tentacles just below the eyes, and discard. The tentacles will be joined together – in the centre is a beak-like mouth, which can be removed by squeezing it out. Slip the fingers under the skin covering the body pouch and peel it off. Cut the fins away from either side of the pouch. Rinse the pouch and dry thoroughly. Finely chop the tentacles.

Heat 1 tablespoon oil in a frying pan, add the spring onions and garlic and cook, stirring occasionally, for 2–3 minutes. Add the chopped tentacles and cook for a further 2–3 minutes.

Transfer the mixture to a blender or food processor, add the spinach and mix for about 1½–2 minutes. Season then divide the stuffing between the squid body pouches. Close the openings with wooden cocktail sticks then place the squid close together in a baking dish. Sprinkle with the remaining oil and bake for about 20 minutes. Remove the cocktail sticks and sprinkle the squid with chopped parsley or basil.

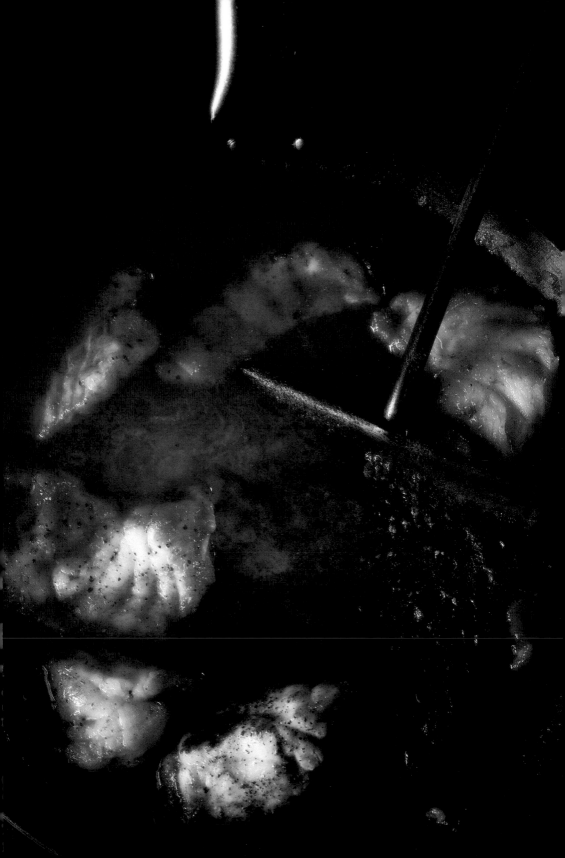

Above: Michel Mioche, chef at the *Hotel Radio* in Clermont-Ferrand preparing his POIRES À LA FOURME D'AMBERT (*see page 187*).

Previous page: LOTTE A L'ARMORICAINE (*see page 86*).

Opposite: SARDINES EN BROCHETTES (*see page 89*). Dipping the sardines in sea salt helps to keep the fish supple and easy to fold on to the skewer.

Provençaux and Provençales sip the sun with infinite
precaution – especially when eating outside.

SHELLFISH

Les Crustacés

· ·

ASSIETTE DE FRUITS DE MER

Seafood platter

A sumptuous platter piled high with many different types of cooked and live seafood and perched on top of a wire stand is a wonderful sight whether it is served as a starter, a main dish at home or a refreshing snack in a brasserie after the theatre.

I remember a glorious Sunday lunch in Roscoff where I sat with three generations of sea- and shellfish-loving people sharing a staggering display. Everyone was as dainty and swift with their tools as medieval craftsmen. Tiny fingers catching winkles briskly, big fingers cracking claws vivaciously. With perseverance and anticipation they attacked everything from the tiniest grey shrimps to the fiercest looking crabs, extracting delicate pieces, chewing, biting, sucking and cracking enthusiastically. As they enjoyed the messy, fragrant, traditional Sunday ritual, sharing tools, memories and jokes, there was plenty of time to see how the meal made them close to each other.

Whether the seafood is cooked or live, make sure it is all really fresh; if it is cooked it should, of course, still be in its shell. Ideally, there should be a choice of different types of oysters and clams, but away from the coast this is not always possible. The time of year will also affect and influence the selection of fish in an *Assiette*.

Don't forget to put the paraphernalia of crab pickers, nutcrackers, tiny forks and pins as well as finger bowls and paper napkins on the table.

SHELLFISH

—————— *Serves 4* ——————

12–16 clams

12–16 mussels

12 Dublin Bay prawns

1–1¹/₂ lb (450–750 g) prawns

about 12 oz (350 g) brown shrimps

about 1 lb (450 g) cockles and winkles

8–12 oysters

1 cooked crab, shell cracked (see page 101)

FOR THE BROTH

3 pints (1.75 litres) water

salt

10 fl oz (300 ml) dry white wine

1 small onion, studded with 1 clove

2 bay leaves

2 sprigs thyme

6 black peppercorns

TO SERVE

fresh seaweed or cracked ice

thinly sliced rye and country bread

slightly salted butter

Mayonnaise (see page 47) or
    Aïoli (see page 48)

lemon quarters

Leave the clams and mussels for 2–3 hours in a large basin or bucket of heavily salted cold water, stirring occasionally with a wooden spoon to get rid of the sand.

Put all the ingredients for the broth into a large saucepan, bring to the boil then boil gently for 10 minutes. Add the Dublin Bay prawns and simmer for 2¹/₂ minutes. Add the prawns, cook for 2 minutes, add the shrimps and cook for a further 2 minutes. Remove all the prawns and shrimps using a sieve or slotted spoon, and leave to drain. Add the cockles and winkles to the pan and poach for 4 minutes. Remove and drain. Reserve the pan of broth.

Scrub the clams and mussels with a hard brush under cold running water. Discard any that are not tightly closed, or have damaged shells. Remove and discard the 'beards' from the mussels. Remove the onion from the broth then pour off all but 5 fl oz (150 ml). Bring the broth remaining in the pan to the boil, add the mussels, and clams that are to be eaten cooked, cover and cook over a high heat, shaking the pan occasionally, for about 5 minutes until the shells have opened. Drain, discard any shells that have remained closed, then leave to cool.

Open the clams that are to be eaten raw, and the oysters (see page 106) just before serving. Line a large plate with seaweed or cracked ice and arrange all the seafood on it.

Place thinly sliced rye and country bread, unsalted butter, a bowl of Mayonnaise or *Aïoli* and plenty of lemon quarters on the table.

CRABES À LA MAYONNAISE
Crab mayonnaise

One of the most enjoyable ways of spending an early morning or late afternoon is to visit the harbour at Guilvinec or Concarneau when the fishing boats return with their catches. Crates and baskets filled with scallops, conger eels, rock salmon (dog fish), lobster and crabs are carried to the other side of the quay where, at the *marché à la criée*, wholesale fish market, the auctioneer calls for bids on the lots and the customers respond in all kinds of peculiar ways: wriggling their nose, rubbing their ears, shaking their thumbs or raising their eyebrows. A little later the local fish market opens in the square for the villagers. Although the amount and variety of fish and shellfish every day is staggering, crabs, particularly *tourteaux*, common crabs, are the most abundant and the most reasonable in price. Other crabs may be *araignées*, spider crabs, which, as their name suggests, have long, thin legs, and small *étrilles*, fiddler or velvet crabs.

Crabs are available all year round but are at their best during the summer. Choose crabs that smell fresh and feel heavy for their size. If buying a cooked crab, which many people prefer to do, keep it cool and eat it on the same day.

In Brittany, and elsewhere, crab is often preferred to lobster, and there is no better way of enjoying it than this simple recipe. Don't forget to have on the table all the necessary paraphernalia – nutcrackers, crab pickers, pins stuck on corks, and last but not least, finger bowls with lemon slices floating in them.

—————— *Serves 4* ——————

4 freshly-boiled crab, each weighing about 1 lb (450 g)
2 tablespoons whipping cream
Lemon Mayonnaise (see page 48)
1 tablespoon finely chopped fresh chives, parsley and chervil
pinch cayenne pepper

Vinaigrette (see page 47)

TO SERVE
fresh seaweed, cracked ice or crisp salad leaves
thinly sliced country bread
slightly butter

Place one crab on its back. Twist the claws backwards and break them from the body. Remove the legs in the same way, snapping them loose at the lowest joint, as close as possible to the shell. Crack the claws into large pieces with a blow with the back of a heavy knife, but take care not to crush the meat inside. Lift the pointed apron flap, or tail, break it away from the body and discard it. With the point of a sharp knife, prise up the central part of the shell, then pull it free. Discard the spongy gills (dead men's fingers) from the sides of the main body section. Also discard the small bag-like stomach sack and the attached threads, situated near the crab's mouth. Crack the central section in half, if liked. Repeat with the remaining crabs.

Place all the pieces of crab on a bed of seaweed, ice or crisp salad leaves. Lightly whip the cream, then lightly fold into the Mayonnaise. Gently stir in the herbs and add cayenne pepper, to taste. Serve this sauce, the Vinaigrette, thinly sliced country bread and slightly butter with the crab.

MOULES ET PALOURDES FARCIES

Stuffed mussels and carpetshell clams

Palourdes, which grow to 3 inches (7.5 cm), are the largest of the European clams that are considered worth eating. They can be eaten raw, like oysters, or cooked in the same way as mussels. Also, like mussels, they are grown off the coasts of Brittany and the Vendée and there are a number of different recipes for stuffing them. Serve the stuffed mussels or clams piping hot with thin slices of crusty bread to mop up the juices.

———————— *Serves 4* ————————

4 lb (2 kg)/4 pints (2.25 litres)
   mussels or clams
salt
10 fl oz (300 ml) water
3 sprigs thyme

FOR THE CREAM AND CHEESE STUFFING
2 oz (50 g) butter

1 large shallot, finely chopped
4 fl oz (120 ml) double cream
4 oz (100 g) Gruyère cheese, grated
approximately 1 oz (25 g) fresh
   breadcrumbs
3 tablespoons finely chopped fresh,
   flat-leaved parsley

Discard any mussels or clams that are not tightly closed or are damaged. Scrub the mussels or clams under cold running water, using a hard brush. Place in a sink or bowl of salty water, discard any that float, then leave the others for 2–3 hours to remove all the sand. Drain the mussels or clams and rinse again. Remove the stringy 'beards' from mussels.

Bring the water to the boil in a large saucepan. Add the thyme and mussels or clams, cover tightly and cook over a high heat, shaking the pan from time to time, for about 5 minutes until the shells open. Strain off the liquid. Discard the top shell of each clam or mussel, and any that remain closed.

For the cream and cheese stuffing, pre-heat the grill. Line 4 shallow heatproof dishes with crumpled foil.

Heat half the butter in a frying-pan, add the shallot and cook gently for about 3 minutes. Stir in the cream and bring to the boil. Remove from the heat and stir in the cheese, about three-quarters of the breadcrumbs and the parsley. Using a teaspoon place a little of the mixture around each clam or mussel, sprinkle with the remaining breadcrumbs, and dot with the remaining butter. Arrange in the dishes and place under the grill for 2–3 minutes until brown.

Variations

BACON, TOMATO AND HERB STUFFING	3 tablespoons white wine
1 tablespoon olive oil	1¹/₂ tablespoons finely chopped mixed
1 onion, finely chopped	fresh herbs such as parsley, chervil,
6 oz (175 g) lean streaky bacon	basil and mint
2 oz (50 g) cooked, or raw ham such	salt and freshly ground black pepper
as Bayonne, diced	1 egg, lightly beaten
2 garlic cloves, finely minced	juice 1 lemon
1 large tomato, skinned, seeds	
removed, chopped	

Pre-heat the oven to gas mark 7, 425°F (220°C). Line 4 shallow baking dishes with crumpled aluminium foil.

Heat the oil in a frying-pan, add the onion and cook, stirring occasionally, for 3–4 minutes. Stir in the bacon, ham, garlic and tomato and cook for about 5 minutes. Stir in the wine, herbs, salt and pepper and simmer for 4–5 minutes.

Remove the pan from the heat, and stir in the egg. Fill each mussel or clam shell, arrange in the foil, and bake for about 8 minutes. Drizzle a few drops of fresh lemon juice over and serve.

BUTTER, SHALLOT AND HERB STUFFING	1 teaspoon chervil
4 shallots, chopped	6 oz (175 g) butter, softened
1 garlic clove, chopped	1¹/₂ tablespoons white wine
2¹/₂ tablespoons chopped fresh parsley	salt and freshly ground black pepper

Pre-heat the oven to gas mark 8, 450°F (230°C). Line 4 shallow baking dishes with crumpled foil.

Place the shallots, garlic, and herbs in a blender or a food processor and mix briefly. Place the butter in a bowl, add the shallot mixture, wine and seasonings, and beat together. Spoon a little of the butter around each clam or each mussel in its half shell, place in the dishes and bake for 3–4 minutes.

MOULES MARINIÈRES

Mussels cooked in white wine and herbs

The best mussels are *bouchots*, so called because they attach themselves to, and grow on, wooden posts, *bouchots*, erected by fishermen in the water along many stretches of the French coastline. There are many different recipes for cooking them but this light, fresh-tasting mussel dish is popular everywhere. Mussels should be tightly closed before they are cooked and they must be eaten the same day they are bought. Cooked mussels which are not open should be discarded.

———— *Serves 4 as a first course* ————

4 lb (2 kg)/4 pints (2.25 litres) mussels	1 sprig thyme
	parsley stems
2 oz (50 g) butter	salt and freshly ground black pepper
2 tablespoons oil	3 tablespoons chopped, fresh flat-leaved
1 clove garlic, crushed	parsley
3 shallots or ½ onion, finely chopped	
½ pint (300 ml) dry white wine	TO SERVE
1 bay leaf	rye or wholemeal bread and butter

Scrub the mussels with a hard brush, under running cold water, then place in a sink filled with cold salted water and discard those which float or are not tightly closed. Leave for 2–3 hours. With a knife or with your fingers pull out the 'beards' which come out of each shell then rinse well under cold running water until the water is free of sand and the shells are clean.

Heat the butter and oil in a very wide frying-pan or saucepan. Add the garlic and shallots or onion and cook gently for 3–4 minutes until soft. Pour in the wine and bring to the boil. Add the herbs, salt and mussels, cover and cook for about 5 minutes, shaking the pan, and tossing it with an up-and-down motion twice so that the mussels cook evenly. The shells should all be open; discard any that remain closed. Scoop out the mussels with a wide, flat, draining spoon, and place them in a warm, deep dish. Discard the empty top half of each shell using oven gloves. Cover the dish and keep the mussels warm.

Strain the cooking liquid through a sieve lined with a double thickness of cheesecloth. Rinse the pan, return the liquid to it, bring to the boil then boil for 5 minutes. Pour over the mussels and sprinkle with pepper and chopped parsley. Serve at once in warm soup plates, with rye or wholemeal bread and butter.

Variations

*For a richer dish, the cooking liquid can be reduced over a high heat for 10 minutes then 5 or 6 tablespoons of double cream and lemon juice to taste stirred in before pouring onto the cooked mussels.

* Cider may be used instead of wine if you want to make *Moules Marinières* following a Brittany or Normandy recipe.

* Diane and Alexandre Faidy, aged four and six, who made *Moules Marinières* for me in Roscoff, did not use garlic, bay leaf and thyme.

VENDÉE

HUÎTRES CHAUDES

Warm oysters with cream and chives

Traditionally, oysters are eaten raw with buttered bread and a squeeze of lemon juice, or a drop of vinegar as we do in Paris, but today warm oysters bathed in either a light or a rich sauce are becoming fashionable.

On the island of Oleron we ate the celebrated green *Marennes* oysters with crisp, hot sausages and drank *Pineau de Charente*, a fortified wine produced not far away in the region that makes Cognac. It was an overwhelming experience.

The easiest way to prepare warm oysters is to nestle them on their half shells in a $^1/_2$ inch (1 cm) layer of coarse sea salt, rock salt or sand so they will not slip, then place them in an oven pre-heated to gas mark 4, 350°F (180°C) for 3 minutes and serve with a bowl of whipping cream or soured cream and a large peppermill. But my favourite way is this very special recipe from Valentin Brun, chef of *La Marée*, one of La Rochelle's most popular seafood restaurants.

Choose oysters that are very fresh, very full, heavy and tightly closed. Unopened oysters can be kept deep-shell down and wrapped in a damp cloth, so they stay moist, in the refrigerator or in a cool place for four to five days; do not put them in water. Once opened, oysters must be eaten as soon as possible.

Writing in the early nineteenth century Brillat-Savarin, the famous

gourmet, recorded when referring to oysters that 'In the old days,...
there were a good many guests who did not stop before they had
swallowed a gross (144)' and he reports seeing one man eat 32 dozen
(384). Six to twelve per person is usually adequate nowadays although
for the following recipe, four oysters per person should be enough as the
topping is luxurious.

———————— Serves 4 ————————

16 plump oysters
1 oz (25 g) butter
1 shallot, very finely chopped
6 fl oz (175 ml) crème fraîche
2 tablespoons lemon juice
2 tablespoons finely chopped
  fresh chives
salt and white pepper

FOR THE LEEKS
1 oz (25 g) butter
white part 1 small, slim leek, finely
  chopped
1 tablespoon chopped chives

Pre-heat the oven to gas mark 4, 350°F (180°C). Line a shallow baking
dish with crumpled foil.

Rinse the oyster shells. Cover one hand with a thick cloth, then
place the oyster, rounded-side down, in your palm. Insert a strong knife
with a short, pointed blade where the growth rings start in the shell,
alongside the hinge. Holding the two halves of the oyster together, give
the knife a quick upward turn, cutting through the muscle at the hinge.
Slide the knife under the oyster to cut it free from the shell. Discard the
top shells and the liquor. Place the oysters in the dish and put in the oven
for about 3 minutes.

For the leeks melt the butter in a small saucepan, add the leeks and
cook gently until softened, stir in the chives. Remove from the heat and
keep warm.

Melt the butter in a small frying-pan, add the shallot and cook over
a moderate heat, stirring occasionally, for about 4 minutes until softened. Stir in the crème fraîche and boil for 2–3 minutes until lightly
thickened. Add the liquid from the oysters, the lemon juice, chives, salt
and pepper, and simmer for 1–2 minutes. Spoon a bed of leeks and chives
into each oyster shell and place the oysters on top. Spoon the shallot
mixture over each oyster then place in the oven for a few minutes.

Using oven gloves place the oysters in their shells on a plate lined
with a napkin or coarse salt so they will not slide.

SALADE DE COQUILLES ST JACQUES
Scallop salad

Fashions for recipes come and go, but I have loved this one for a long time and use it often as the ingredients are neither overly rare nor expensive. From October until May, when fresh scallops are available, this is one of the quickest and easiest recipes to prepare. I serve the scallops either on a bed of crisp lettuce leaves, such as batavia (escarole) or a bed of chicory, lightly cooked in butter for 15 minutes.

———— *Serves 4* ————

1 head batavia (escarole)
16 scallops on the half-shell
2 oz (50 g) butter
1 teaspoon vegetable oil
salt and freshly ground black pepper
juice 1 lemon
1 large avocado pear
2 tablespoons chopped fresh chervil,
  thyme or flat-leaved parsley

FOR THE DRESSING
5 tablespoons mixed olive oil and
  vegetable oil
2 tablespoons white wine vinegar
1 tablespoon double cream
salt and freshly ground black pepper

Stir the dressing ingredients together in a bowl, or shake them together in a screw-top jar. Wash and trim the batavia (escarole) and separate the leaves. Place on a large flat plate.

Use a sharp knife to sever the scallops from their shells and separate the corals from the white bodies. Discard the membrane surrounding the corals and bodies, and the dark organs and crescent-shaped muscles from the bodies. Rinse and pat dry.

Heat the butter and oil in a wide frying-pan, add the scallops and corals and cook for $1^{1}/_{2}$ minutes on each side. Using a fish slice, remove from the pan, sprinkle with salt, pepper and lemon juice, then using a sharp knife, thinly slice each body; leave the corals whole. Scatter the scallop slices and corals over the batavia (escarole).

Quickly peel the avocado, cut in half, discard the stone and slice the flesh. Arrange the slices around the plate. Shake or stir the dressing then pour over the salad. Scatter the chervil, thyme or parsley on top. Take to the table and toss just before serving.

*E*SCARGOTS À LA *B*OURGUIGNONNE

Snails with parsley and garlic butter

There are two main types of snails eaten in France, the little grey ones, *petits gris*; and the large, brownish *escargots de Bourgogne*, which are generally considered to be the best variety.

The Romans loved snails and centuries later, during the Middle Ages, monasteries and convents had snail parks but it was not until the end of the nineteenth century that snails really became a popular food in France. Today it is estimated that an average French person eats 1½–2 lb (750 g–1 kg) a year. However, a large majority of these snails are imported, mainly from eastern European countries, because the native snail population is declining. When imported snails have been cooked according to any traditional French recipe they become, if not quite the brothers of French snails, at least their well-meaning cousins.

Serves 4–6

24 large, or 36 small canned snails, drained and rinsed

FOR THE FILLING
8 oz (225 g) butter
3 garlic cloves, finely chopped
1 shallot, finely chopped
3 tablespoons finely chopped fresh parsley

salt and freshly ground black pepper
juice 1 lemon
4 tablespoons dry white wine

TO SERVE
thin slices of bread

Pre-heat the oven to gas mark 7, 425°F (220°C). Line 4 individual baking dishes with crumpled foil, unless you have a special snail plate.

Mix together the butter, garlic, shallot, parsley, salt, pepper and lemon juice. Using a small teaspoon or the tip of a knife, place a little butter mixture in each snail shell. Place the snails back in the shells and place a little more of the butter mixture on top. Put the snails on their snail cooking plate or in the dishes. Spoon a little wine over each snail and bake for about 5 minutes. Serve hot with thin slices of bread.

POULTRY

Les Volailles

●●●●●●●●●●●●●●●●●●●●●●●●●●●●

POULET AU VINAIGRE

Chicken with cucumber in vinegar and cream sauce

Poulet au Vinaigre is a delicious dish which is popular throughout France, but this is my favourite version: a free-range chicken, good red wine vinegar and a fiery Dijon mustard will ensure this *Poulet au Vinaigre* is a sumptuous treat. Serve with rice or noodles and braised fennel, buttered broad beans or sautéed, grated courgettes

———————— *Serves 4* ————————

2 tablespoons vegetable oil

1 oz (25 g) butter

3½–4 lb (1.5–1.75 kg) free-range
  chicken, cut into 8 pieces

2 extra chicken breast
  portions (optional)

salt and freshly ground black pepper

2 garlic cloves, finely chopped

2 shallots, finely chopped

1 onion, finely chopped

4 tablespoons red wine vinegar

1 tablespoon brandy

8 fl oz (250 ml) dry white wine

1 cucumber, peeled, halved lengthways,
  seeds removed, cut into ½ inch
  (1 cm) dice

3 tablespoons Dijon mustard

3 tablespoons double cream

1½ tablespoons chopped mixed fresh
  herbs such as chives, dill or parsley

Pre-heat the oven to gas mark 6, 400°F (200°C).

Heat the oil and butter in a large, heavy-bottomed frying pan. Season the chicken then add the legs to the pan and cook for about 15 minutes, turning occasionally with tongs, until they are golden on all sides. Transfer to a shallow, ovenproof dish, cover with foil and place in the oven. Cook the chicken breasts in the pan for about 10 minutes until evenly browned then add to the legs. Cover the dish again and leave in the oven with the heat switched off.

Discard half of the fat from the pan, add the garlic, shallots and onion and cook for 4–5 minutes until soft. Pour the vinegar, brandy and wine into the pan and bring to the boil, scraping up the coagulated juices from the bottom with a wooden spoon. Add the cucumber and simmer for 10 minutes. Stir in the mustard, lower the heat then stir in the cream. Add the chicken pieces, turn in the sauce to coat them then cook gently for 10–15 minutes. Check the seasoning then sprinkle with the herbs. Serve from the casserole or transfer to a warm, shallow dish.

─────── **BURGUNDY** ───────

POULET AU FROMAGE

Chicken with cheese, wine and vegetables

This recipe was inspired by a former mayor of Dijon, Monsieur Gaston Gérard. He deglazed the juices of a sautéed chicken with white wine, then covered the bird with a rich sauce of cream and mustard, before baking it until crisp. I have made it many times, each time experimenting with different vegetables and spices. Now, with an interesting combination of leeks, celeriac and ginger, this is my favourite chicken recipe. It is rich and delectable.

I serve *Poulet au Fromage* for a buffet as it keeps warm in its baking dish, for an elegant dinner because it is easy to serve and needs only a little tossed salad for an accompaniment, and for an informal lunch.

─────────── *Serves 4* ───────────

3 tablespoons groundnut oil

1 oz (25 g) unsalted butter

1 large free-range chicken, cut into
    8 pieces

2 extra chicken breasts (optional)

salt and freshly ground black pepper

1 small celeriac bulb

2 leeks, white part only, sliced

2 stalks celery cut into 1 inch
    (2.5 cm) pieces

10 fl oz (300 ml) dry white wine

7 fl oz (200 ml) whipping cream

2 tablespoons Dijon mustard

1½ tablespoons finely chopped
    fresh ginger

pinch freshly grated nutmeg

pinch cayenne pepper

6 oz (175 g) Gruyère cheese, grated

3 tablespoons fresh breadcrumbs

Pre-heat the oven to gas mark 5, 375°F (190°C).

Heat 2 tablespoons oil and half the butter in a wide frying-pan and cook the chicken pieces, in batches, skin side down first, for about 10 minutes or until brown. Turn them over and cook the other side for another 10 minutes. Transfer the chicken pieces when they are browned to a heavy casserole. Sprinkle with salt and pepper.

Meanwhile, peel the celeriac and cut into 1 × 1 inch (2.5 × 2.5 cm) cubes and cook in boiling, salted water for about 8 minutes. Heat the remaining oil and butter in a frying-pan and cook the leeks and celery, stirring occasionally, for 4–5 minutes. Add to the casserole with the drained celeriac.

Spoon off excess fat from the frying-pan, then pour in the wine and scrape up the coagulated juices at the bottom with a wooden spoon. Bring to the boil and boil for 2–3 minutes. Remove from the heat, cool slightly then stir in the cream, mustard, ginger, nutmeg, cayenne pepper and two-thirds of the cheese. Pour over the chicken and vegetables. Sprinkle over the breadcrumbs and the remaining cheese. Cover with foil and bake for 20 minutes. Remove the foil and cook for another 20–25 minutes until the top is brown.

——————— BURGUNDY ———————

*P*OULET À LA *C*RÈME ET AUX *M*ORILLES

Chicken with cream and morel mushrooms

Arguably the best chickens in the world come from the Bresse area of Burgundy. These very special birds can be identified in the shops by the Government-regulated *label rouge* on them. This guarantees that the white-feathered, blue–grey legged Bresse breed of chicken have been raised according to strict controls that specify the area of open space they must be given in which to roam, define a diet containing plenty of corn and milk, and state the minimum age at which the birds can be killed. Real devotees of Bresse chicken only eat them roasted to fully savour their pure flavour, but the following dish is also very popular, especially on the menus of *ferme-auberges*, farms in France which serve their own products, in this case, chickens. I tasted one version on the Perrin family's *ferme-auberge, Les Plattières*. The elder Madame Perrin was responsible for looking after the chickens, protecting them from foxes and buzzards, checking the quality of the grass, feeding them corn and monitoring them in the cooking pot.

For my luxurious version, do try to use the best quality free-range chicken you can find. Morel mushrooms are very expensive and rarely

Opposite: Vaucluse, Provence. A paradise on earth: mountains, orchards, wild flowers and exotic trees; the Provence of the Impressionists.

Above: Argentan on the River Orne in Normandy.

Opposite: Pointe de Penmarch in Brittany: granite roofs and
billowing clouds.

available fresh so are more often used in their dry form. These are sold in packets of about ³/₄ oz (20 g) and although these may also seem expensive, they are highly-flavoured and a few go a long way. I add fresh mushrooms for extra texture.

───────────── *Serves 4* ─────────────

³/₄ oz (20 g) dried morels
2 tablespoons vegetable oil
¹/₂ oz (15 g) butter
3 lb (1.5 kg) free-range chicken, cut up into 8 pieces
8 oz (225 g) fresh mushrooms
approximately 15 fl oz (450 ml) chicken stock (see method)

2 tablespoons brandy
4 fl oz (120 ml) double cream
juice 1 lemon
salt and freshly ground black pepper

TO GARNISH
chopped fresh parsley

Put the morels into a small bowl. Just cover with boiling water and leave to soak for 30 minutes.

Meanwhile, heat the oil and butter in a heavy casserole, add the chicken in batches and cook over a moderate heat for about 10–15 minutes until evenly browned. When the chicken is brown, transfer to a warm plate, cover and keep warm. Add the fresh mushrooms to the casserole and fry for 4–5 minutes, stirring occasionally. Remove using a slotted spoon. Discard any fat left in the casserole then return the chicken and fresh mushrooms to it.

Remove the morel mushrooms from the soaking liquid. Pour the liquid through a sieve into a measuring jug and add enough chicken stock to bring the liquid up to 1 pint (600 ml) and pour over the chicken. Wash the morels again to get rid of any remaining sand. Add the mushrooms to the chicken, cover and simmer gently for about 40 minutes or until the chicken is completely cooked.

Remove the chicken from the casserole, cover and keep warm. Add the brandy to the casserole, bring to the boil quickly and continue to boil for 2–3 minutes. Add the cream and lemon juice, and boil until the liquid is thickened and rich-tasting. Season then return the chicken pieces to the casserole and heat through for about 5 minutes. Serve sprinkled with chopped parsley.

Opposite: Pont l'Abbé, Brittany where lace caps are the region's traditional dress.

POULE AU POT FARCIE

Poached stuffed chicken

Henri IV was a liberal king and flexible about many things. He changed his religion from protestant to catholic in order to keep France united, and although he married quite young, he retained an active interest in the opposite sex all his life. One point on which he was to remain utterly inflexible, though, was his wish that each family in his kingdom should have a poached chicken every Sunday. This was a good way of cooking older hens that had stopped laying eggs so were no longer useful, as the long, slow, gentle cooking tenderised their flesh. Every region has its own recipe for the stuffing, but whether the chicken is filled with country ham and spinach, as in the following recipe, with pork and chopped cabbage, a spicy sausage, onion and parsley mixture, or with a mixture containing plenty of vegetables, it is always welcome at family meals. The ritual of serving and eating the dish has varied little over the years: first, the broth is served on Croûtons (see page 70) sprinkled with fresh herbs, then the carved chicken and the stuffing are served with the vegetables and a bowl of well-flavoured Vinaigrette (see page 47).

I like to cook the vegetables separately as I think their crisper textures and fresher flavours are more appealing than vegetables cooked in the pan with the chicken. I spoon a little hot broth over the steamed vegetables before serving the dish. The combination of fragrant chicken, tasty stuffing and fresh vegetables is truly a winning one.

———————— *Serves 6–8* ————————

FOR THE STUFFING
1¹/₂ tablespoons vegetable oil
2 medium onions, chopped
4 oz (100 g) chicken livers, chopped
8 oz (225 g) frozen chopped spinach,
    thawed, drained and squeezed dry
1 lb (450 g) lean streaky bacon, or
    raw ham, coarsely chopped
4 cloves garlic, chopped
10 sprigs flat-leaved parsley, chopped
4 shallots, chopped
1 tablespoon fresh thyme
pinch freshly grated nutmeg
2 eggs, lightly beaten
salt and freshly ground black pepper

FOR THE CHICKEN
4¹/₂ lb (2 kg) free-range chicken
¹/₂ oz (15 g) butter
2 tablespoons groundnut oil
1 bay leaf
2 sprigs thyme
1 onion, halved, each half studded with
    1 clove

salt
5 black peppercorns
2 additional large chicken legs
    (optional)
2 tablespoons finely chopped fresh
    chives or flat-leaved parsley

FOR THE VEGETABLES
Choose as large a selection as you like.

8 carrots, halved lengthways and cut
    into 2 inch (5 cm) pieces
4–8 small purple turnips, depending on
    size, halved or quartered
8 leeks, white part only, split
    lengthways, cut into 4 inch (10 cm)
    pieces, and tied into a bundle with a
    piece of string
4 onions, halved
4 bulbs fennel, cut in half lengthways
8 stalks celery, into 2 inch (5 cm)
    lengths

TO SERVE
double quantity Vinaigrette (see
    page 47)

To make the stuffing heat the oil in a frying-pan and sauté the onions for 3–4 minutes. Add the chicken livers, stir with a wooden spoon for 1 minute then remove from the heat. Stir in the spinach, bacon or ham, garlic, parsley, shallots, thyme, nutmeg, eggs and salt and pepper. Spoon into the cavity of the chicken, making sure it is not tightly packed. Sew up the opening, and truss the bird so that it will not lose its shape during cooking.

Heat the butter and 1 tablespoon oil in a large frying-pan over a fairly high heat, add the chicken and brown lightly all over. Remove from the heat and place in a large saucepan. Add the bay leaf, thyme, onion halves, salt and peppercorns, cover with water, cover the pan and bring slowly to the boil. Immediately lower the heat so the liquid barely simmers and cook gently for 1¹/₄ hours.

Add a little more oil to the frying-pan and fry the chicken legs, if using, until lightly browned. Add to the saucepan. If cooking the vegetables with the chicken, add them as well. Cook for a further 45 minutes.

If you prefer to steam the vegetables, about 30 minutes before the chicken is cooked bring a saucepan of water to the boil. Put the vegetables in a steaming basket, cover and place over the saucepan. Cook for 15–20 minutes until tender – if necessary, they can continue to cook while you carve the chicken.

Carefully remove the chicken and the legs, if using, from the saucepan. Discard the chicken skin, if liked, then remove the stuffing and place on a warm plate. Carve the chicken and add to the plate. Spoon over a few tablespoons of hot broth, and sprinkle with chives or parsley. Place the vegetables on another warm plate; spoon a little hot broth over steamed vegetables and season with salt and pepper. Pour some of the remaining broth into a hot sauceboat or jug and serve with the bowl of Vinaigrette, the chicken and the vegetables.

Variation

Add 2 chopped hard-boiled eggs to the Vinaigrette.

— **THROUGHOUT FRANCE** —

Coq au Vin

Chicken cooked in red wine

Coq au Vin is one of the most enduring of the great traditional dishes. It is served in many different settings – country inns, small bistros, grand restaurants, family homes – yet no one ever tires of it. As it simmers on the stove, anguish and any worries which may linger on your mind fade away within minutes.

It is an old dish. It may be as old as our Gallo-Roman civilisation. According to the legend, when the cheeky, prosperous Gauls were besieged by the Romans they sent them an insolent *bon appétit*! message hung around the neck of one of their thinnest and most scrawny chickens. Julius Caesar, an astute man, decided that if the making of fine roads and good laws had not yet convinced the Gauls of the Romans' abilities he would try another route. He invited them to join him for dinner and served the rooster metamorphosed into a succulent, tasty dish by long simmering in Roman wine and herbs. The Gauls took one bite, then another, and concluded that the Romans were at long last displaying some sign of civilisation. Hence the beginning of a long lasting relationship.

To be truly authentic, a cockerel should, of course, be used, but though it is difficult for most of us to find a mature cockerel today we can compensate by marinating a free-range chicken overnight in red wine and cooking it in a very flavourful wine-based sauce. I usually cut the chicken into pieces and add extra breasts to make sure there are plenty of meaty portions as they absorb the juices so much better.

Opinions vary about what wine to use: some people say it should be a good one, others advise that it should be a simple, hearty wine. I have tried both and my vote lies with the latter.

The chicken can be cooked in the wine and broth or stock up to a day or so in advance, cooled and kept in the refrigerator. Reheat it over a low heat for about 40 minutes, then proceed with the recipe, thickening the liquid and adding the vegetables and bacon.

With *Coq au Vin* I like to serve a Vegetable Purée such as Celeriac or Fennel (see pages 160–161), tiny steamed potatoes, rice or noodles to absorb the sauce, and a large bowl of a tossed salad to refresh the palate.

——————— *Serves 6* ———————

4¹/₂ lb (2 kg) free-range chicken (with
    giblets), cut into 6 joints
2 extra chicken breasts (optional)
salt and freshly ground black pepper
2 tablespoons fresh thyme
¹/₂–1 oz (15–25 g) butter
2–3 tablespoons vegetable oil
4 oz (100 g) thick-cut lean streaky
    bacon, diced
12 oz (350 g) button onions or
    shallots, peeled
2 carrots, thickly sliced
2 stalks celery, cut into ¹/₂ inch
    (1 cm) cubes
8 oz (225 g) button mushrooms
2 bay leaves
2 sprigs parsley
1 sprig thyme
1 large onion, sliced
1 tablespoon plain flour beaten with ¹/₂
    oz (15 g) unsalted butter
1–2 tablespoons brandy
the chicken's liver, finely chopped
3 cloves garlic, crushed
2 tablespoons double cream
pinch freshly grated nutmeg
juice 1 lemon

FOR THE MARINADE
1 pint (600 ml) red wine
1 onion, sliced
1 carrot, sliced
2 bay leaves
2 cloves garlic, crushed
2 sprigs thyme
10 black peppercorns
2 tablespoons olive oil

FOR THE BROTH
¹/₂ pint (300 ml) chicken stock
or
chicken neck, bones and giblets, except
    the liver
1 onion, stuck with 1 clove
1 bay leaf
salt
1 sprig thyme
4 black peppercorns
1 pint (600 ml) water

TO SERVE
2 slices bread, made into Triangular
    Garlic-flavoured Croûtons
    (see page 85)
2 tablespoons finely chopped
    fresh parsley

Combine all the ingredients of the marinade in a saucepan. Bring to the boil, lower the heat and simmer for 10 minutes. Cool.

Place the pieces of chicken in a single layer in a large, flat, non-metallic dish. Pour over the cold marinade, cover and leave in the refrigerator overnight, turning the chicken 2 or 3 times.

If you do not have a good chicken stock available, put the other ingredients for the broth into a large saucepan and simmer, uncovered, for 30 minutes, skimming the scum from the surface occasionally. Correct the seasoning, pour through a sieve then measure ¹/₂ pint (300 ml). Discard the contents of the sieve.

Lift the pieces of chicken from the marinade and pat dry with paper towels. Reserve the marinade liquid, vegetables and herbs. Sprinkle each piece of chicken with salt, pepper and thyme.

Heat ½ oz (15 g) butter and 2 tablespoons oil in a large, heavy-bottomed frying-pan. Add the chicken legs and thighs, skin-side down, and cook over a high heat until crisp and golden, turn over and brown the other side. Transfer to a heavy flameproof casserole. Add the breasts to the pan, skin-side down, and cook for 2 minutes, turning them over halfway through, and adding a little more butter if necessary. Transfer to the casserole.

Add the streaky bacon to the frying-pan, adding more oil if necessary, and cook until crisp and brown. Remove and set aside. Add the button onions or shallots, carrots and celery to the pan and cook for 4–5 minutes, turning them with a wooden spoon. Remove the vegetables and set aside. Add the mushrooms to the pan for a few minutes. Sprinkle them with salt, remove from the pan and set aside.

Remove as much fat as you can from the surface of the liquid left in the frying-pan and pour any remaining cooking juices into the casserole. Pour in the reserved marinade liquid, vegetables and herbs, and the chicken stock or broth. Bring just to simmering point, lower the heat and add the herbs and sliced onion. Cover and simmer gently for about 45 minutes, until the chicken is tender and the juices of the chicken run clear when you prick the thickest parts with a fork.

Transfer the pieces of chicken to a warmed serving dish. If you dislike skin, discard it. Cover the chicken and keep warm. With a spoon remove and discard the fat from the surface of the cooking liquid. Gradually whisk in the flour and butter mixture then boil until lightly thickened. Add the carrots and celery. Lower the heat and simmer for 10 minutes. Return the pieces of chicken to the casserole, cover and cook gently for 10 minutes. Dip one corner of each Croûton into the *coq au vin* sauce, then into the chopped parsley.

Discard the bay leaves, parsley and thyme sprigs from the casserole. Stir in the brandy, chicken liver, bacon, mushrooms, button onions or shallots, garlic and cream. Add nutmeg, lemon juice, salt and pepper to taste, cover the casserole and cook for 2 minutes. It is ready. Transfer to the serving dish and place the Croûtons around the edge.

*P*INTADE AU *P*ORTO, *P*OMMES ET *P*OIRES

Guinea fowl braised in port, with apples and pears

The flesh of guinea fowl is dark red and lean. When cooked in port with apples, pears and onions, it makes an elegant dish with a hint of the wild. I like to serve this dish with Celeriac Purée (see page 161), Cabbage Purée (see page 161), sautéed chestnuts, sautéed mange-touts, cabbage simmered in butter, or steamed rice. Alternatively, it can be accompanied by a simple, tossed chicory or watercress salad.

———————— *Serves 4* ————————

2 teaspoons chopped fresh thyme	*2 apples, peeled, cored and*
salt and freshly ground black pepper	*thickly sliced*
3 lb (1.5 kg) guinea fowl	*1 pear, peeled, cored and thickly sliced*
1¹/₂ oz (40 g) unsalted butter	*4 tablespoons port*
2 tablespoons groundnut oil	*12 pearl onions*
2 thin slices streaky bacon	*3 tablespoons double cream*

Place a pinch of salt, the thyme and ¹/₂ oz (15 g) butter in the cavity of the bird. Rub the breast, back and legs with ¹/₂ oz (15 g) butter and 1 tablespoon oil and season the skin with salt and pepper. Truss the bird with string so that it keeps its shape while cooking and lay the streaky bacon over the breast.

Heat the remaining butter and oil in a heavy casserole, add the bird and brown on all sides for a few minutes, then cover and cook, basting occasionally with the cooking juices, for 25 minutes. Add the apples, pear and port and cook over a low heat for about 25 minutes.

Meanwhile, simmer the onions in lightly salted water for about 10–15 minutes, until tender. Drain well and add to the casserole with the cream. Cover and cook for a further 5 minutes.

Transfer the guinea fowl to a warm plate. Cut and discard the strings holding the bacon in place. Cover the bird and leave in a warm place to 'relax' for 5–10 minutes. Cut the pieces of bacon in 1 inch (2.5 cm) pieces. Check and correct the seasoning of the apples and pear.

Carve the guinea fowl and arrange the slices on a warm plate. Spoon over the bacon, apples, pear and onions and half of the cooking juices. Serve the remaining juices in a warm bowl.

PROVENCE

PIGEONNEAUX AUX OLIVES

Pigeon with olives

Beware if a man calls you his 'little pigeon', the word 'little' may be misleading: it's time to lose weight!

I usually use tender, plump farm-bred pigeon. A three to four month old bird, sometimes called 'squab', weighs 1 pound (450 g) and is generally enough for two people but you may prefer to serve one pigeon per person. Pigeons need fat to protect them as they cook. You can coat them with butter, but I prefer to wrap them in larding fat or bacon. This dish is lovely with sautéed mushrooms, peas cooked with lettuce leaves and diced bacon, or any potato dish.

Serves 2 or 4

2 young pigeons, each weighing about 1 lb (450 g)
salt and freshly ground black pepper
1 tablespoon fresh thyme
2 bay leaves
4 slices streaky bacon
1 tablespoon vegetable oil
1 oz (25 g) butter
3 fl oz (75 ml) sweet white wine

2 shallots, finely chopped
8–16 large green olives, stoned
1 large tomato, skinned, seeds removed, diced
3 tablespoons water
1/2–1 lemon, thinly sliced
2 tablespoons finely chopped fresh parsley

Season the outside of the birds with salt, pepper and thyme. Place a little salt, pepper and 1 bay leaf in the cavity of each bird. Truss them then wrap individually in 2 bacon slices. Tie the bacon in place with string.

Heat the oil and butter in a heavy casserole over a moderate heat. Add the pigeons and cook for about 10 minutes until evenly browned.

Pour in the wine and scrape up the coagulated cooking juices with a wooden spoon as best you can. Cover and cook for 30 minutes over a low heat, turning the birds a few times using tongs.

Cut the strings holding the bacon in place and remove both the strings and the bacon. Add the shallots to the casserole, cook for 2 minutes, add the olives and tomato and cook for 10 minutes. Transfer the pigeons to a warm dish, cover and keep warm. Remove and discard the fat on top of the cooking juices with a spoon. Stir the water into the casserole, scraping up the coagulated juices. Bring to the boil, simmer for 2–3 minutes then add the lemon slices and parsley. Cover the casserole and keep warm.

Cut each pigeon in half lengthways, pour over the cooking juices and surround the pigeons with olives and lemon slices.

— **THROUGHOUT FRANCE** —

CAILLES AU GENIÈVRE ET AU COGNAC

Quails with thyme, juniper berries and brandy

Lucky quail: to be plump has always been considered a virtue for this bird. But the quails of yesterday are not the quails of today. While once upon a time a quail wrapped in bay leaves or in a fresh vine leaf and plainly roasted exploded with flavours, the little farmed quails we find today are bland. Amusing, crisp, pretty perhaps, but they do need a little help from the cook to improve their charms. After trying the usual ploys – cherries, quinces, grapes, mushrooms and even a few small pieces of truffle, my solution is now quite definite: I add a pungent twist to quails by cooking them with thyme, juniper berries, shallots and brandy. Serve the sauce in a separate bowl so both the toasted bread and the birds will remain crisp. One quail per person should be just enough if the accompaniment is quite generous. I serve either sliced fennel sautéed in butter, Fennel Purée (see page 160), or *Gratin de Pommes de Terre* (see page 171).

—————— *Serves 4* ——————

12 juniper berries	*2–4 shallots, very finely chopped*
12 black peppercorns	*2 tablespoons brandy*
salt and freshly ground black pepper	*1 tablespoon finely chopped*
4 quails	*fresh parsley*
1 oz (25 g) butter, softened	
3 tablespoons chopped fresh thyme	*TO SERVE*
8 thin slices streaky bacon	*1 lemon, thinly sliced*
4 slices firm bread, buttered,	*watercress*
crusts removed	

Preheat the oven to gas mark 8, 450°F (230°C).

Place 3 juniper berries, 3 peppercorns and a pinch of salt in the cavity of each quail. Spread butter over each bird then sprinkle with pepper and thyme and wrap in two slices of bacon. Tie these in place with string.

Place each bird on a slice of bread and place in a small roasting tin. Bake for 15 minutes.

Transfer the quails on their pieces of bread to a warm serving plate, discard the strings holding the bacon in place, cover and keep warm.

Stir 4 tablespoons water into the cooking juices then add the shallots and simmer for about 2 minutes. Stir in the brandy and parsley, bring to the boil, then simmer again for about $1\frac{1}{2}$–2 minutes. Check the seasoning, and pour into a warm bowl. Garnish the serving plate with lemon slices and watercress.

CANETON RÔTI ET SA FARCE

Roast duck with spinach stuffing

In France many types of duck are sold, such as Muscovy with their generous amounts of firm breast meat, large Barbary and the smaller, more tender and delicately-flavoured Nantais or Challans. Now, these are becoming more widely available in Britain, and there are also two special breeds of British duck that have a higher than average proportion of flesh to fat, Lunesdale and the larger Gressingham.

A stuffed duck can be delicious, but it can also be unpleasantly greasy. To be sure of a successful dish, roast the bird for quite a long time, prick it frequently to get rid of most of the fat, and cook the stuffing separately. Also, of course, use the best duck you can.

Sautéed diced turnips or a simple, crisp, green salad make a good accompaniment.

———— *Serves 3* ————

4½–5 lb (2–2.25 kg) duck, preferably
   fresh, thawed if frozen
1½ tablespoons chopped fresh thyme
juice 1 lemon
salt and freshly ground black pepper
2 garlic cloves, halved
2 bay leaves
5 tablespoons dry white wine
1 tablespoon brandy
3–4 spring onions, with 1 inch (2.5
   cm) green, cut in half lengthways
15–24 large green olives, stoned
2 teaspoons finely grated lemon rind

FOR THE STUFFING
1 tablespoon groundnut oil
1 garlic clove, chopped
duck's liver, if available, chopped
7 oz (200 g) frozen spinach, thawed,
   well-drained and chopped
4 tablespoons cooked rice
1 large egg, lightly beaten
3 tablespoons chopped fresh
   flat-leaved parsley
2 teaspoons chopped fresh thyme
pinch grated nutmeg
salt and freshly ground black pepper

Pre-heat the oven to gas mark 8, 450°F (230°C). Butter a 4½ inch (12 cm) round, or 2 × 3½ inch (5 × 9 cm) china or earthenware dish.

Remove as much fat and excess skin from the neck and tail end of the duck as possible. Sprinkle thyme, lemon juice and salt and pepper on the skin and put the garlic cloves and bay leaves in the cavity. Season inside the bird with salt, then truss it and prick the breasts and legs several times with a fork. Put on a rack placed in a roasting tin. Roast in the oven for 20 minutes, then pour as much fat as you can from the tin. Lower the oven temperature to gas mark 4, 350°F (180°C) and cook for a further $1^1/_4$–$1^1/_2$ hours until the juices between the legs and breasts run pale yellow.

Meanwhile, prepare the stuffing. Heat the oil in a frying-pan, add the garlic, and liver, if available, and sauté for 2–3 minutes. Stir in the spinach and cook for 2–3 minutes, then stir in the rice, egg, parsley, thyme and nutmeg and season with salt and pepper. Spoon into the dish, cover tightly with foil and place on the shelf below the duck when the temperature is at the lower setting. Cook for about 40–45 minutes.

Transfer the rack with the duck on it to a plate and leave to 'rest' in the oven with the heat turned off and the door slightly ajar. Spoon or pour off surplus fat from the roasting tin then stir the wine, brandy, spring onions and olives into the tin, scraping up the coagulated juices with a wooden spoon. Simmer on the hob for a few minutes. Stir in the grated lemon rind, salt and pepper.

Carve the duck and arrange on a warmed serving plate. Unmould the stuffing, cut into slices and arrange with the duck. Spoon the sauce over the duck and stuffing.

DINDONNEAU AUX MARRONS

Roast turkey with mushroom, chestnut and olive stuffing

Dodu dindon (plump turkey), or *jesuit*, because it was imported from North America by the Jesuits in the seventeenth century, roast turkey is the traditional family dish for Christmas and New Year's Eve throughout France. In the following recipe the roast, stuffed bird is served with sautéed chestnuts and crisp sausages. To accompany the bird I serve a bowl of watercress tossed with an olive oil and lemon juice dressing. If you are using a frozen turkey, leave it in its plastic wrapping in the refrigerator for 2 days to thaw.

Serves 6–8

7 lb (3 kg) turkey, with giblets
salt and freshly ground black pepper
3 tablespoons groundnut oil
1 lb (450 g) mushrooms, quartered
3 oz (80 g) butter
3 shallots, finely chopped
1 lb (450 g) streaky bacon, finely diced
4 oz (100 g) green olives, stoned and
    halved or quartered
2 tablespoons brandy (optional)
10 walnut halves, roughly
    chopped (optional)
2 tablespoons finely chopped
    fresh parsley
1 tablespoon fresh thyme

1 egg, beaten
8 oz (225 g) peeled, cooked chestnuts
    (see page 159), or whole chestnuts
    canned in brine or water, drained
12 fl oz (350 ml) dry white wine

FOR THE GARNISH
1 tablespoon vegetable oil
2 long, thin, tasty sausages
6 oz (175 g) peeled and cooked
    chestnuts (see page 159), or whole
    chestnuts canned in brine or
    water, drained
1½ oz (40 g) unsalted butter
2 tablespoons finely chopped
    fresh chervil

Pre-heat the oven to gas mark 9, 475°F (240°C).

Remove the giblets from the turkey. Rinse and thinly slice the heart, rinse and dice the liver. Wash the bird inside and out and dry carefully. Sprinkle salt and pepper over the skin and in the cavity.

Heat 2 tablespoons oil in a frying-pan, add the mushrooms and sauté for 3–4 minutes. Using a slotted spoon, transfer to a bowl. Add half the butter and the remaining oil to the pan and sauté the shallots for 1½ minutes, stirring with a wooden spoon. Add to the bowl. Add the bacon to the pan and cook for 3–4 minutes. Add the heart, sauté for 1 minute then add the liver. Toss everything with a wooden spoon, remove from the heat and stir. Add to the bowl with the olives, brandy and walnuts if using, the parsley, thyme, egg and salt and pepper. Stir well. Halve or quarter the chestnuts, if liked, then stir into the bowl.

Spoon loosely into the turkey's neck cavity as the stuffing will swell as it cooks. Fold the neck skin over the stuffing and sew it in place, or secure it with skewer. Spoon the remaining stuffing into a small baking dish and cover with foil.

Truss the bird and spread the remaining butter over the surface of the breast, back and legs. Place the turkey on a rack, breast-side up, in a large roasting tin, cover the bird with a piece of buttered or oiled foil, or, better still, a large piece of muslin dipped in vegetable oil, to keep it moist while it cooks. Place in the oven, lower the oven temperature to gas mark 8, 450°F (230°C) and roast for 30 minutes. Lower the temperature to gas mark 6, 400°F (200°C) and pour 1 pint (600 ml) water into the roasting tin to prevent the juices burning and smoking. Cook for another 1–1¼ hours. Put the dish of stuffing in the oven. Remove the foil or the muslin from the turkey and cook for a further 30 minutes until the juices run pale yellow when you test the thickest part of the leg with a fine skewer.

Transfer the cooked turkey to a warm plate and discard the trussing string or skewers. Cover the bird loosely and leave in a warm place for 20–30 minutes.

For the garnish, heat the oil in a frying pan, add the sausages and fry, turning occasionally, for about 5 minutes, until crisp and brown. Meanwhile, toss the chestnuts in butter over a moderate heat for about 5 minutes then sprinkle with the chervil.

To serve, remove the stuffing from the turkey with a tablespoon and place it in the centre of a warm serving plate. Remove the legs and the wings then cut each leg into 2 joints. Slice the breasts and arrange around the stuffing. Cut the sausages into 2 inch (5 cm) lengths and place on the plate with the chestnuts.

Carefully spoon or pour the fat from the roasting tin, then stir the wine into the pan, scraping up the sediment with a wooden spoon. Boil for 1–2 minutes on the hob, season lightly, spoon some over the stuffing and turkey and pour the remainder into a sauceboat.

───────── **ALSACE** ─────────

OIE AUX POMMES ET AUX PRUNEAUX

Roast goose with apple and prune stuffing

Prunes, apples and goose do go wonderfully together. In Alsace, the home of this recipe, beer is sometimes massaged into the skin of the goose before cooking for extra flavour. Keep the fat that comes from the goose to use for frying vegetables, especially potatoes.

Serve the goose with chestnuts or potatoes sautéed in goose fat, or a selection of Vegetable Purées (see page 158).

───────── *Serves 6–8* ─────────

20 no-need-to-soak prunes
9 lb (4 kg) goose, with giblets, thawed in the refrigerator if frozen
1 oz (25 g) butter
1 tablespoon vegetable oil
2¹/₂ inch (6 cm) thick slices lean streaky bacon, diced
3 onions, or 4 shallots, finely chopped

5 apples, such as Granny Smith, peeled, cored and quartered
2 tablespoons brandy (optional)
grated rind 1 lemon
2 teaspoons dried thyme
1 egg, lightly beaten
salt and freshly ground black pepper
freshly grated nutmeg
14 fl oz (400 ml) Alsace Riesling

Opposite: CANETON ROTI ET SA FARCE (*see page 124*)

Above: The solid architecture of Burgundy is reflected in its hearty cooking.

Right: AGNEAU AUX HERBES (*see page 132*)

Above: Strasbourg, Alsace. A region which reflects its historical switching of nationality between France and Germany.

Pre-heat the oven to gas mark 7, 425°F (220°C). Place a wire rack in a roasting tin.

Place the prunes in a bowl, cover with hot water and leave for about 30 minutes, then drain, carefully remove the stones and cut the prunes into quarters.

Meanwhile, pull out as much fat as you can from inside the goose. Reserve the fat (see Note). Remove the giblets from the bird's cavity and reserve the liver for the stuffing.

Melt ½ oz (15 g) butter and the oil in a frying-pan, add the bacon and sauté, stirring occasionally, for 5 minutes. Using a slotted spoon transfer to a bowl. Add the goose liver to the pan and cook, stirring, for about 2 minutes. Using a slotted spoon remove the liver, chop it and add to the bowl. Add the onions or shallots to the pan, sauté for 3 minutes, then add to the bowl.

Add the remaining butter to the pan. When hot add the apples and cook for 2–3 minutes, stirring. Add the brandy, if using, and set alight with a lighted taper. When the flames have died down, tip into the bowl with the lemon rind, thyme, prunes, egg, salt and pepper. Grate over a little nutmeg and stir to mix.

Prick the thighs, back and lower breast of the goose with a sharp fork. Season the cavity with salt and pepper then spoon in the apple and prune mixture. Sew up the opening carefully and truss the goose. Sprinkle salt and pepper on the outside of the bird then place, breast uppermost, on the rack in the roasting tin. Roast for 30 minutes then turn the bird on its side. Lower the oven temperature to gas mark 4, 350°F (180°C), and place a baking tin of hot water in the bottom of the oven as the steam will keep the bird moist during cooking. Cook the goose for 30 minutes, baste with a little boiling water and turn the goose onto its other side. Remove the melted fat from the roasting tin using a spoon or bulb-baster and put into a dish. Roast the bird for a further 30 minutes, baste again and turn the bird on its breast. Once more, remove surplus fat from the roasting tin and cook the bird for another hour until the juices run pale yellow when you test the thickest part of the leg with a fine skewer. Remove excess fat from the roasting tin during the hour, if necessary. Switch off the oven, leave the oven door open and allow the goose to 'relax' for 20–30 minutes.

Discard the trussing strings from the goose. Spoon the stuffing into the centre of a warm serving plate. Cut off the legs and separate the drumsticks from the second joints. Slice the breast, and the second joints.

Arrange the pieces of goose around the stuffing.

Carefully pour or spoon all the fat from the roasting tin, leaving the juices and sediment behind, then place the tin on the hob. Stir the wine into the coagulated juices, scraping up the sediment with a wooden spoon, then boil for 2–3 minutes. Season with salt and pepper and spoon some of the sauce over the goose and stuffing; serve the remaining sauce separately.

Note

Chop the fat from the goose then place it in a small saucepan with a little water. Cover and simmer gently for a few minutes. Remove the lid from the pan and continue to cook until the water has evaporated. Carefully pour the fat through a sieve into a jar or bowl leaving any sediment in the pan. Leave to cool then cover the jar or bowl. Keep in the refrigerator.

MEATS

Les Viandes

●●●●●●●●●●●●●●●●●●●●●●●●●●●●●●●

AGNEAU AUX HERBES

Lamb with herbs and garlic

Fontvieille is a pretty village near Arles. Nearby are fragrant fields of rosemary and thyme, Daudet's windmill, sheep and goats roaming on terraced pastures, Roman arenas and olive groves. The village houses have long, narrow, wooden shutters and rust-coloured tiles; the little village square, with its green iron tables and chairs, is sheltered by huge plane trees. It is inland Provence at its best and everybody seems to follow the lizard's advice engraved on fountains and sundials all around 'I sip life as I sip the sun, by small gulps. Time passes too fast, perhaps it will rain tomorrow'. Taking the time to enjoy life is a priority.

In the centre of the village is a pretty restaurant situated in a disused oil mill and built around a lovely Provençal garden. It is called *La Regalido*, the Provençaux word for the log of wood which is added to the fire as a welcome when guests arrive.

Hospitality, warmth and pleasure in all the good things of the land were all present as we entered the kitchen of *La Regalido* that morning. There was a big bundle of freshly-gathered thyme sprinkled with blue blossoms, piles of fresh vegetables, a stack of flat vegetable omelettes ready to be made into an omelette cake. Monsieur Jean-Pierre Michel was stuffing a chicken with a handful of thyme and 40 garlic cloves, his son was making a thyme sorbet while Madame Michel was making bouquets of flowers. Busy lizards but true lizards. Monsieur Michel made me taste a crisp vegetable *gratin* ('in Paris they would add cream to it, here we only want the concentrated flavours of the garden'), a bite of a tiny purple artichoke that had been cooked briefly in herbs and wine, a morsel of peppery sheep's milk cheese, and an explosive paste of anchovies, oil and garlic as he talked to me about olives and described how local bakers used to crack the stones and place them in the bottom of their ovens to flavour their breads. When the *Agneau aux Herbes* arrived I truly felt like a pampered lizard. As you will see yourself it is very easy to prepare, but the meat must be chosen carefully. It can be served with a *Gratin de Pommes de Terres* (see page 171), *Gratin de Courgettes* (see page 167) or *Ratatouille* (see page 154). Glorious every time. *Allez zou*, let's go, as they would urge in Fontvieille.

———— *Serves 4* ————

4 thick lamb leg steaks or cutlets	*3¹/₂ tablespoons olive oil*
1 teaspoon finely chopped	*16 garlic cloves*
fresh rosemary	*1¹/₂ oz (40 g) unsalted butter*
1 tablespoon chopped fresh thyme	*salt and freshly ground black pepper*

Place the lamb in a dish. Sprinkle over half of the thyme and rosemary and 1 tablespoon olive oil. Turn the lamb over and sprinkle with the remaining herbs and another tablespoon of olive oil. Cover and leave to marinate for about 2 hours.

Thread the garlic cloves onto 4 wooden cocktail sticks. Heat 1¹/₂ tablespoons olive oil and half the butter in a heavy-bottomed frying-pan. When it is very hot, add the lamb and cook quickly for about 3 minutes turning frequently with tongs until evenly browned on all sides. Lower the heat to moderate. Sprinkle the lamb with salt and pepper, and add the remaining butter to the pan. When it begins to sizzle add the garlic cloves and cook until tender and evenly browned.

Transfer the lamb and garlic to 1 large, or 4 individual, warm plates and pour over the cooking juices.

*B*LANQUETTE DE *V*EAU

Veal casserole with mushrooms, pearl onions and cream

There are a great many ways of making a *blanquette*. In Paris, and in fashionable restaurants, it is a very white and delicate dish, in Brittany it is enhanced by cider and served with artichokes, and in some country kitchens it is prepared the way I saw when I visited Madame Léa Lajudie on her family's cattle farm outside Limoges – the veal was sautéed in oil then some vegetables and herbs added, but no cream or egg yolks were included.

I have used the following recipe for *Blanquette de Veau* for a long time. It is pungent and light, yet also unctuous and exquisite.

Selecting the correct meat is important. The veal must be whitish–pink in colour with enough bones and cartilage left in the neck or breast to provide flavour and to thicken the sauce. You may need to order the veal specially from your butcher. A *blanquette* is usually served with plain rice or tiny new potatoes. It is also good with steamed asparagus, braised chicory, sliced artichoke hearts, tiny broad beans or mange-touts.

─────────── *Serves 4–6* ───────────

2 lb (1 kg) breast or neck of veal, cut
    into 2 inch (5 cm) lean pieces
1 lb (450 g) boned shoulder of veal,
    cut into 2 inch (5 cm) pieces
1 cracked veal bone (optional)
salt and freshly ground black pepper
½ pint (300 ml) dry white wine
1 large onion, studded with 4 cloves
1 large clove garlic, peeled
350 g (12 oz) button mushrooms,
    divided into stems and caps
2 sprigs parsley
2 bay leaves
3 sprigs thyme

1 long strip lemon rind
2 oz (50 g) butter
2 tablespoons flour
1 tablespoon vegetable oil
3 carrots, sliced
12 pearl onions, fresh or frozen, or
    spring onions with about 1 inch
    (2.5 cm) green stem
juice 2 lemons
2 egg yolks
5 fl oz (150 ml) double cream
1 teaspoon freshly grated nutmeg
1 teaspoon grated lemon rind
2 tablespoons chopped fresh chervil or
    flat-leaved parsley

Place all the veal and bones in a large saucepan. Sprinkle with salt, cover with cold water and bring slowly to the boil, skimming off the scum as it rises to the surface. Continue to boil gently for 30 minutes, removing the scum as it appears. Add the wine, onion, garlic, mushroom stalks, parsley, bay leaves, thyme and strip of lemon rind to the pan, cover and simmer very gently for 1 hour. Uncover and cook for a further 30 minutes. Lift out the meat and bones using a slotted spoon. Pour the liquid through a sieve placed over a deep bowl. Discard the lemon rind and herbs from the sieve and press the vegetables through the sieve into the liquid. Return the liquid and sieved vegetables to the saucepan and bring to the boil. Continue to boil until 18 fl oz (550 ml) is left.

Melt 1 oz (25 g) butter in a small saucepan, stir in the flour and cook, stirring, for about 2 minutes. Remove from the heat and gradually stir in about half of the hot broth. Return to the heat, bring to the boil, stirring, then simmer for about 5 minutes. Stir into the pan of broth and cook for another 5 minutes. Add the veal, carrots and pearl or spring onions, cover and simmer gently, stirring from time to time, for about 15 minutes, until the carrots and onions are tender.

Meanwhile, heat the remaining butter and the oil in a frying-pan and fry the mushroom caps on all sides for 3–4 minutes. Sprinkle with salt and pepper, then add the juice of 1 lemon and cook for about 2 minutes more.

Stir the egg yolks and cream together then stir in a little of the hot broth. Stir this mixture into the pan of veal, vegetables and broth over a very low heat. Add the nutmeg, grated lemon peel, remaining lemon juice and salt to taste. The sauce should be silky and highly flavoured. Sprinkle with fresh chervil or flat-leaved parsley.

Variation
In Provence, lamb is used for a *blanquette*.

ESCALOPES VALLÉE D'AUGE

Veal escalopes with mushrooms, wine and cream

The cooking of Normandy is based on cattle, cider or Calvados, and rich cream, all of which are used in this typical regional recipe. Serve with Fennel Purée (see page 160), potatoes, Vegetable Timbales (see page 163), buttered, steamed rice or a simple watercress salad.

Serves 4

4 veal escalopes, each weighing about
    4 oz (100 g)
salt and freshly ground black pepper
1½ oz (40 g) butter
1 tablespoon groundnut oil
6 oz (175 g) mushrooms, sliced
1 tablespoon Calvados

10 fl oz (300 ml) dry white wine
6 fl oz (175 g) whipping or
    double cream

TO GARNISH
sprigs flat-leaved parsley

Place the veal between two sheets of greaseproof paper or cling film and pound with a mallet or a rolling pin until they are about ¼–½ inch (5 mm–1 cm) thick. Discard the paper or cling film. Season the veal on both sides with salt and pepper.

Heat ½ oz (15 g) butter and the oil in a large frying-pan over a moderately high heat. Add 2 escalopes to the pan, cook briskly for 2 minutes, turn over and cook for a further 2 minutes. Transfer to a warm plate, cover and keep warm. Cook the remaining 2 escalopes in the same way and transfer to the plate.

Add the remaining butter to the pan and sauté the mushrooms for 5 minutes, stirring occasionally with a wooden spoon. Add to the veal on the plate.

Stir the Calvados and wine into the pan, scraping up the sediment with a wooden spoon. Bring to the boil then simmer for 4–5 minutes. Stir in the cream and simmer for another 4–5 minutes. Slide the veal and mushrooms back into the pan, cover and cook gently for 2–3 minutes. Season to taste.

Lift the veal onto a warm serving plate and spoon over the mushrooms and sauce. Garnish with parsley sprigs.

Variations

* The veal escalopes can be replaced by veal chops, or chicken breasts, but the cooking time should be 20–25 minutes over a moderate heat.
* You can also add 2 finely chopped shallots with the calvados.

—————— LIMOUSIN ——————

FOIE DE VEAU À LA MOUTARDE

Calves liver with mustard and wine sauce

In Auvergne I ate venison liver enriched with cream and mustard, I ate slices of delicate goose liver on cooked apples in Alsace, and in Provence, pork liver with onions, but calves liver as I tasted it in Limousin remains, for me, the most flavourful of them all.

Liver must be carefully trimmed so there are no nerves or membranes, and cooked within a day of buying it. The slices can be very thin or very thick; I like them to be at least $^1/_2$ inch (1 cm) thick. Serve this recipe with Celeriac Purée (see page 161), Vegetable Timbales (see page 163), *Pommes Frites* (see page 174) or with a crisp, tossed salad

——————— *Serves 4* ———————

1 lb (450 g) calves liver, sliced
salt and freshly ground black pepper
2 tablespoons flour
2 oz (50 g) butter
2 tablespoons vegetable oil

2 shallots, sliced, or 4 spring onions
sliced lengthways
4 tablespoons dry white wine
2–3 teaspoons Dijon mustard
1 tablespoon finely chopped fresh flat-
leaved parsley

Sprinkle both sides of the slices of liver with salt and pepper and dust lightly with flour.

Heat $1^1/_2$ oz (40 g) butter and 1 tablespoon oil in a frying-pan. When it is very hot, sauté the liver for about 1 minute on each side, depending on the thickness. Remove to a warm plate, cover and keep warm.

Add the remaining butter and oil to the pan and sauté the shallots or spring onions for 2–3 minutes. Stir the wine then the mustard into the pan, then add salt and pepper and the parsley. The sauce will thicken a little. Pour over the liver and serve at once.

DAUBE AUX OLIVES

Beef stew with olives

This is one of the oldest Provençal dishes and most local cooks have their own distinctive ways of achieving perfection. For example, the meat may be sautéed before being cooked in the wine or it may be put directly into the cold wine, pork rind, salt pork, a calf's foot or cap mushrooms may be added. The only golden rule they all share is that the *Daube* must cook very slowly for a long time so that the meat is tender and the flavours mingle perfectly. Traditionally plump, earthenware *daubières* were used. These are now difficult to find but a *Doufeu* makes an excellent substitute.

A *Doufeu*, a sturdy, enamelled cast-iron casserole with a shallow lid that is filled with cold water so the aromatic steam rising from the casserole is quickly condensed and drips on to the meat and vegetables to keep them moist, is wonderful for this type of stew.

The following recipe is my favourite, but the *Daube* prepared near Nyons by Madame Hélène Charrasse-Moinier was superb, especially as not only were her daughter and grand-daughter helping, but her husband made the best *Tapenade* (see page 49) in Provence to be added as a final touch to the piping hot stew.

Serve the *Daube* with buttered macaroni, noodles, new potatoes or ravioli (in Nice, *Daube* is used with Swiss chard to stuff the ravioli as well), or with a tossed green salad.

Serves 6–8

8 oz (225 g) lean salt pork or streaky
    bacon, diced
1 onion, chopped
2 tablespoons olive or groundnut oil
2¹/₂ lb (1.25 kg) chuck steak, cut into
    2 inch (5 cm) cubes
salt and freshly ground black pepper
1 pint (600 ml) hearty red wine
6 medium tomatoes, coarsely chopped
3 carrots, sliced

3 sprigs fresh thyme or marjoram
1 clove
2 inch (5 cm) wide strip orange rind
    dried in an oven or the open air
3 cloves garlic
2 bay leaves
2 tablespoons Tapenade (see
    page 49)
2 tablespoons chopped fresh flat-leaved
    parsley

Sauté the pork or bacon and the onion in the oil in a thick-bottomed frying-pan for 5 minutes, stirring once or twice. Add some of the beef to the frying-pan and sauté on all sides for about 8 minutes until lightly browned. Sprinkle with salt and pepper then transfer the beef, onions and pork or bacon to a large, heavy casserole. Add the wine to the casserole, cover and start to cook over a low heat.

Meanwhile, sauté the rest of the beef in several batches, adding the pieces as they are cooked to the casserole. Sprinkle a little salt and pepper on top, add the tomatoes, carrots, garlic, bay leaves, thyme, clove, orange rind, and enough water to cover the meat. Cover tightly and simmer very gently for $3^1/_2$ hours. Stir in the *Tapenade*. Correct the seasoning, remove and discard the bay leaves, thyme or marjoram and the orange rind, then sprinkle finely chopped parsley evenly over the *Daube*.

Note
The *Daube* may also be cooked in an oven set to gas mark 1–2, 275–300°F (140–150°C).

The flavour of the *Daube* will improve if it is cooked a day in advance and reheated. Follow the recipe as far as the addition of the carrots, but instead of adding them, leave the *Daube* to cool and keep in a cold place overnight. About 45 minutes before the meal, heat to simmering point, stirring frequently, add the carrots and continue with the recipe.

A teaspoon of red wine vinegar may be added to the wine to help tenderise the meat.

Variation
To make *Daube en Gelée*, Jellied Beef Stew, add a split pig's trotter or a large piece of pork rind to the *Daube*. After it has been cooked, arrange the carrots, olives and bay leaves in the bottom of a bowl and carefully spoon over the rest of the *Daube*. Cover and leave in a cool place to set. To unmould, wrap a warm towel around the bowl for a few minutes, then invert the bowl on to a cold plate.

BOEUF BOURGUIGNON

Burgundy beef casserole with button onions and mushrooms

Each region has its own definite interpretation of beef stew. Burgundy's version, with bacon, button onions and mushrooms is probably the most famous of them all. It is better if this dish is prepared ahead of time so you have time to skim off the excess fat and to allow all the flavours to develop. It can be served just with a salad of chicory or endive and watercress, or rocket and batavia (escarole), with *Vinaigrette* (see page 47), and good bread; or with tiny new potatoes boiled in their jackets or noodles, and Celeriac Purée (see page 161) and sautéed carrots.

—————————— *Serves 6* ——————————

2¹/₄ lb (1.1 kg) chuck steak, cut into
   1¹/₂ inch (4 cm) cubes
3 tablespoons vegetable oil
2 cloves garlic, crushed
1¹/₂ tablespoons plain flour
1 tablespoon brandy
salt and freshly ground black pepper
8 oz (225 g) piece lean streaky bacon,
   cut into ¹/₂ inch (1 cm) dice
12 oz (350 g) button onions or shallots
4 oz (100 g) button mushrooms
2 tablespoons chopped fresh flat-leaved
   parsley

FOR THE MARINADE
1 onion, sliced
1 carrot, sliced
1 stalk celery, chopped
salt and freshly ground black pepper
1 pint (600 ml) hearty red wine,
   preferably Burgundy
2 cloves garlic, crushed
1 bay leaf
3 sprigs thyme

Place the pieces of beef in a large bowl, add all the ingredients for the marinade, stir then cover and keep in the refrigerator overnight or for a whole day.

Remove the pieces of meat from the marinade and dry with paper towels. Strain the marinade and reserve the liquid, carrot and onion. Heat 2 tablespoons oil in a heavy casserole and sauté the meat, a few pieces at a time, for about 10 minutes, until brown on all sides. Turn the pieces carefully using tongs or a wooden spoon. As the beef is cooked, transfer to a bowl using a slotted spoon.

When all the meat is browned, add the reserved onion and carrot, and the garlic to the casserole and cook, stirring occasionally, until browned. Return the meat, and any juices that have collected in the bowl, to the casserole. Sprinkle over the flour, then stir in the brandy and reserved marinade liquid. Add the salt and pepper and bring to just below simmering point. Cover tightly and cook very gently for 2 hours.

Heat the remaining oil in a frying-pan, add the bacon and button onions or shallots and cook, stirring occasionally, until lightly browned. Using a slotted spoon, transfer to the casserole. Add the mushrooms to the pan and cook, stirring a few times, for 2–3 minutes. Add to the casserole, cover and cook for a further hour. Remove any fat from the surface and sprinkle over the chopped parsley.

Note

Boeuf Bourguignon can also be cooked in an oven pre-heated to gas mark 1, 275°F (140°C), for the same length of time.

The stew can also be cooked as far as the preparation of the bacon, shallots and mushrooms a day ahead. Cool it quickly and keep it in a cool place. Remove fat from the surface before continuing with the recipe.

BOEUF À LA FICELLE
Poached beef

Chez Camille is a pretty restaurant in Arnay-le-Duc, a small town in the centre of a region where they know how to enjoy *le bien vivre*, good life. I remember the rich polished wood counter, the faded green wicker chairs, the four foot high display of white lilacs, the dazzling selection of perfect dry and fresh goats' cheeses, the platter of walnuts and grapes, the sparkling sky-light above the dining room, the inspired chef-patron, Armand Poinsot, and, behind it all, in time-honoured fashion, his vivacious, cheerful, pretty, efficient wife, Monique. Somehow she managed to keep an eye on the flowers, an eye on the immaculate tables, an eye on their three-year old daughter, and an eye on the splendid Charolais cattle, poultry and vegetable garden she and her husband keep so they have at hand top quality ingredients (and because they give such pleasure), yet still greet customers as if they were her one and only concern in life.

Monique took me for a walk in the fields nearby and we saw her memorable Charolais bull, which weighed about 1200 kg (540 lb), her beautiful creamy cows and her snowy white Bresse chickens. After a day of such physical delights the *Boeuf à la Ficelle* Armand cooked for dinner was as I expected – delicious. With the beef Armand served little crisp croquettes flavoured with plenty of mustard.

Boeuf à la Ficelle is a simple recipe requiring no more than adding tender, well-flavoured beef to a mustard-enhanced broth and cooking it briefly so it remains almost rare inside.

——————— *Serves 4* ———————

1 lb (450 g) sirloin of beef, cut across into 4 slices	2 potatoes cut into large chunks
2 carrots, halved lengthways, cut into 2 inch (5 cm) lengths	¹/₂ cabbage, separated into leaves
	1 tomato
	3 pints (1.75 litres) water
1 stalk celery, halved lengthways, cut into 2 inch (5 cm) lengths	2 bay leaves
	2 sprigs thyme
	2 tablespoons Dijon mustard
	6 black peppercorns
	salt

FOR THE MUSTARD CROQUETTES
2 oz (50 g) good, firm bread without
    crusts, crumbled or crumbed
5 tablespoons milk

2–3 teaspoons Dijon mustard
salt
1 egg white
vegetable oil, for frying

With the point of a sharp knife, make a hole through each piece of beef, near one edge. Pass a long piece of string through each hole. Tie the ends of the strings to a carving fork so the meat can be suspended in a saucepan without touching the bottom. Keep the beef to one side.

Place the herbs, peppercorns, carrots, celery, potatoes and cabbage in a saucepan of boiling water, place the tomato on top and boil for 10 minutes. Strain off the cooking fluid, make up to 3 pints (1.75 litres) with water and put into another saucepan with the mustard and salt. Keep the vegetables warm. Bring the mustard liquid to the boil, add the beef tied to the fork and simmer gently for 5–7 minutes.

Meanwhile, put the bread for the croquettes in a small bowl, sprinkle over the milk and leave for 10–15 minutes.

Drain the vegetables. Place the beef and vegetables on a warm plate, cover and keep warm.

Stir the mustard and salt into the soaked breadcrumbs. Whisk the egg white until stiff but not dry then lightly fold into the breadcrumb mixture. Lightly oil a non-stick frying pan and place over a medium heat. Drop small spoonfuls of the mustard mixture into the pan, taking care not to crowd them. Cook for 1½–2 minutes, until set and golden underneath then turn over and cook on the other side for a further 1½–2 minutes. Transfer to a plate and keep warm while frying the remaining mixture. Serve hot with the beef and vegetables.

Variations

* Leave the beef in one and cook for 15–20 minutes.
* The potatoes, cabbage and tomato can be replaced by 1 onion studded with 2 cloves, a diced, small celeriac bulb and 2 sliced leeks.

POT AU FEU

Boiled meats with marrow bones and vegetables

Pot au Feu is a glorious cousin of *Poule au Pot Farcie* (see page 114), and although described as a dish of boiled meats, bones and vegetables cooked together, the secret of its success lies in the details.

Today every region boasts about its version of *Pot au Feu*. In Provence, lamb, garlic and chickpeas are used, in Auvergne there is pork and cabbage, in Burgundy sausages and stuffed chicken while in Alsace there are *quenelles* (light dumplings) made from the marrow from the beef bones. Other possible additions to *Pot au Feu* can be turkey, partridge, shin of beef, veal knuckle, oxtail, ham, stuffed breast of veal, rabbit or duck portions plus a variety of spices and vegetables. But whether it is an extravagant display or a plain one, *Pot au Feu* remains a most reassuring dish. There is nothing like a steaming *Pot au Feu* to create a feeling of warmth and happiness around a table. It is easy to prepare, is not expensive and does not require much attention. Like all stews, it is at its best if made a day in advance so the fat can be easily removed from the surface, and the flavours allowed to mellow and mature.

Pot au Feu is served in two parts, the broth first with Croûtons (see page 70) and grated cheese, then comes a large plate of boiled vegetables and one of neat, overlapping slices of meats, and a small plate with the marrow bones, more Croûtons, and small spoons for extracting the marrow from the bones.

I prefer to cook the vegetables either in a tiered steamer or in a large pan of boiling water. Celeriac, turnips or parsnips, carrots and potatoes will require 10 minutes longer than the leeks.

Accompaniments could simply be coarse sea salt, gherkins, cherries in vinegar, a pot of mustard or a bowl of horseradish. Or there could be a variety of sauces such as Mayonnaise (see page 47), Aïoli (see page 48) or Vinaigrette (see page 47), according to the occasion and the time available to prepare the meal.

Opposite: BOEUF A LA FICELLE (*see page 142*).

————————— *Serves 8* —————————

1 lb (450 g) bones, such as beef ribs or
veal knuckle
1¹/₂ lb (750 g) piece blade portion of
chuck or top rump tied with a string
like a package
1¹/₂ lb (750 g) piece brisket, tied with
a string
1¹/₂ lb (750 g) short ribs, trimmed

4 carrots, cut in half lengthways, then
in half crossways
4 parsnips or turnips, halved
lengthways
4 leeks, white part only, cut in half
lengthways and tied in a bundle
with a string
4 potatoes, halved

FOR THE BROTH
3 garlic cloves
2 onions, each studded with 2 cloves
1 large leek, chopped
1 carrot, chopped
4 sprigs fresh thyme
2 bay leaves
4 sprigs fresh parsley
10 black peppercorns
salt and freshly ground black pepper
8 pieces marrow bone

TO SERVE
16 round Croûtons (see page 70)
grated Gruyère or Parmesan cheese

FOR THE ACCOMPANIMENTS
Choose two or more from:

coarse sea salt
Dijon mustard
gherkins
Vinaigrette (see page 47) flavoured
with capers, parsley, chopped
shallots and mustard
Herb Mayonnaise (see page 47)
Aïoli (see page 48)

FOR THE VEGETABLES
1 bulb celeriac, quartered

Place the bones, except the marrow bones, in a large saucepan and pile
all the meats on top. Cover with cold water and heat to just on simmering
point. After a few minutes, remove the beige scum that rises to the
surface, using a slotted spoon. Keep doing this until the scum becomes
white and frothy, adding a few tablespoons of cold water twice as you
skim the surface. Add the vegetables, herbs, peppercorns and salt for the
broth. Bring just to the boil then immediately lower the heat, cover and
simmer gently for 2¹/₂ hours.

Scoop the meat and vegetables from the broth and put them on a
plate. Remove and discard the bones. Taste the broth and add salt and

Opposite: POT AU FEU Popular throughout France, this beef
and vegetable dish has many regional variations.

pepper if necessary. Reheat and boil, uncovered, for 5–10 minutes. Pour into a bowl and leave to cool. Cover the meat and vegetables and the broth and refrigerate overnight.

One hour before serving the meal, discard the fat from the top of the broth. Pour the broth into a large saucepan and bring to the boil. If necessary, boil to concentrate the flavours. Add the meat and the vegetables, if liked, and cook over a moderate heat so the liquid just moves, for about 40 minutes.

Meanwhile, pat some salt into the ends of the marrow bones. Wrap them in muslin and tie with a string. Place the marrow bones in cold water, bring to the boil and simmer for 20 minutes. Keep in the water until ready to serve.

Reserve a bowl of hot broth and serve the rest with 8 Croûtons and the cheese. Serve the reserved broth with the meat and vegetables for the second course, along with bowls of the chosen accompaniments.

———— ALSACE ————

BAECKEOFFE

Mixed meat and vegetable casserole

Traditionally *Baeckeoffe* is made with pork and just a small amount of beef, a generous quantity of potatoes and local fruity, dry white wine in a colourful, glazed earthenware dish decorated with flowers. In the days when women in Alsace did all their washing on Mondays they would prepare a *Baeckeoffe* early in the morning, take it to the baker's oven as they walked to the public wash-house, and leave it to be cooked in the dying heat of the bread oven as they did their piles of washing. On their way home they would collect their crisp, tasty casserole.

The very name *Baeckeoffe* is associated with traditional Alsace family life, but the version I ate on a cold spring day at the *Hôtel du Faudé* in Lapoutroie, bore the fresh and imaginative imprint of Thierry Baldinger, a chef who knows his region's dishes but is also aware of his contemporaries' preference for lighter meals. He had used plenty of vegetables, a variety of meats, and most of the fat was removed at the end of the cooking.

It is important to cook *Baeckeoffe* very slowly in a tightly-covered casserole for a long time. A luting paste is often used to seal the lid to the casserole to make sure that the fragrant steam is trapped inside.

———————— *Serves 8* ————————

1 lb (450 g) boneless shoulder of lamb,
   cut into 2 × 2 inch
   (5 × 5 cm) pieces
12 oz (350 g) shoulder of pork, cut
   into 2 × 2 inch (5 × 5 cm) pieces
12 oz (350 g) shoulder or brisket of
   beef, cut into 2 × 2 inch
   (5 × 5 cm) pieces
1 pig's trotter, split (optional)
2 onions, each studded with 2 cloves
4 leeks, white part only, thickly sliced
4 carrots, thickly sliced
2 stalks celery, cut into 2 inch
   (5 cm) lengths
5 tablespoons chopped fresh parsley
2 lb (1 kg) potatoes, cut into ¹/₂ inch
   (1 cm) thick slices

salt and freshly ground black pepper

FOR THE MARINADE
1 carrot, sliced
1 onion, sliced
3 garlic cloves, crushed
4 sprigs fresh thyme
2 bay leaves
salt and freshly ground black pepper
1 pint (600 ml) white wine, preferably
   Alsace Riesling

FOR THE LUTING PASTE
4 tablespoons water
3¹/₂ oz (100 g) plain flour

Place all the meat in a large bowl with all the marinade ingredients. Cover, and leave overnight in a cool place.

Preheat the oven to gas mark 3, 325°F (170°C).

Drain the liquid from the marinade and reserve. Discard the bay leaves. Starting with meat, layer all the marinated ingredients and the fresh ingredients in a large, heavy casserole. Sprinkle salt and pepper on each layer as you go and finish with a layer of potatoes. Pour over the marinade liquid and add water to cover if necessary. Cover with the lid.

To make the luting paste, slowly pour the water into the flour, stirring constantly to make a smooth soft paste; do not beat it. Use to seal the lid to the casserole then cook in the oven for 3 hours.

Break and discard the luting paste. Remove any fat visible on top of the potatoes. Serve from the dish.

Note

Baeckeoffe is even better if cooked a day in advance. About 1 hour before the meal, pre-heat the oven to gas mark 5, 375°F (190°C). Remove the fat from the *Baeckeoffe* then cover the dish and put in the oven for about 30 minutes. Uncover the dish and cook for a further 15–20 minutes.

CHOUCROUTE GARNIE

Alsace sauerkraut and pork

Cabbages grow very easily on the Alsace plain and they are used in many local dishes. However, outside the region the most well-known Alsace way of serving cabbage is *choucroute*, pickled cabbage, called *sauerkraut* in Germany. For generations, preparing *choucroute* has been an important autumnal task. Wooden barrels or stoneware pots are lined with thick cabbage leaves, then the barrel or pot is filled with alternate layers of shredded leaves, coarse rock salt, juniper berries, and bay leaves. A cloth is spread over the top, followed by a heavy lid that is slightly smaller than the mouth of the barrel or pot, then finally a rock or other weight is placed on. At the end of month it is ready for turning into one of Alsace's most celebrated dishes *Choucroute Garnie*. Traditionally this is a hearty dish in which the pickled cabbage is cooked slowly for hours with a wide variety of fresh and cured pork, hams and sausages, but recently I ate the lightest, freshest, most crunchy *Choucroute Garnie* I have ever had. It had been prepared by Madame Colette Faller, at the *Domaine des Capucins*, near Colmar, where she also makes splendid Alsace Sylvaner, Riesling and Gewürztraminer white wines from her own grapes. Madame Faller

cooks the *choucroute* separately from the meats, just bringing them together at the last moment so all the ingredients speak loud and clear. The other keys to a good *Choucroute Garnie* are good, uncooked, or canned or bottled *choucroute*, not using too much wine and cooking it very slowly. Some people in Alsace like to cook it for as long as 8, even 12, hours, some only 2 or 3. Everyone has their own idea of which and how much spices to add. I like to include some carrots for colour as *choucroute* tends to be grey, and I leave the juniper, coriander seeds and the bay leaves to roam freely during the cooking and when I serve the dish. I do not use any goose fat but you may like to add a little with the oil.

A *Choucroute Garnie* for a little dinner or party does not use the same cuts and number of different meats as one for a large family meal. Just bacon, Frankfurters and a smoked sausage can be used or a selection of smoked bacon, green bacon, ham hock, pork knuckle, pork spare ribs, smoked pork shoulder, Frankfurters, large smoked sausages, fresh sausages and black pudding.

—————— *Serves 6* ——————

3 lb (1.5 kg) choucroute, *or canned*
   or bottled sauerkraut
3 tablespoons vegetable oil
1 large onion, sliced
freshly ground black pepper
2 cloves
5 juniper berries, ground
5 coriander seeds, crushed
2 garlic cloves
15 fl oz (450 ml) Alsace Riesling
1 bay leaf
2 carrots, thinly sliced
8 oz (225 g) piece smoked
   streaky bacon
8 oz (225 g) piece green streaky bacon

1 lb (450 g) piece smoked
   pork shoulder
1 pork knuckle
3 large smoked sausages, preferably
   Montbéliard (which are caraway-
   flavoured); or 3 kielbasa or 3
   kabanos
6 Frankfurters
1 blutwurst (blood sausage),
   (optional)
2–3 bratwurst

TO SERVE
Dijon mustard

Rinse the *choucroute* under cold, running water. Drain well, squeeze out excess moisture, then spread on a dish.

Heat 2 tablespoons oil in a saucepan, add the onion and cook over a fairly high heat for 3–4 minutes until soft. Stir in the *choucroute* or *sauerkraut* using a wooden spoon and continue to stir for 5 minutes. Add the pepper, all the spices, the garlic and wine and enough water to cover. Cover and cook over a low heat for about 1 hour 30 minutes, stirring with a fork from time to time. Add the bay leaf and carrots and simmer for 10 minutes.

Meanwhile, place the bacon, smoked pork and pork knuckle in a saucepan, cover with hot water and simmer, allowing 30 minutes per lb (450 g) from when the water reaches simmering point.

Poach the smoked sausages or *kielbasa* for 25 minutes or so then add the Frankfurters and poach for a further 10 minutes. Fry the blood sausage, if using, and *bratwurst* in the remaining oil in a frying-pan for about 5 minutes, turning occasionally.

When everything is cooked, place the *choucroute* or *sauerkraut* on a large, warm plate. Slice the meats and sausages and pile on top of the *choucroute* or *sauerkraut*. Serve with mustard.

Note

Of late, a light version of *choucroute* with fish is being served in some fashionable restaurants, but this is not a new marriage – in the Middle Ages, salmon and even herrings were partnered with *choucroute*. I prefer the union of *choucroute* with pheasant and apples. Two chopped apples can also be added to the *Choucroute Garnie* recipe.

CHEVREUIL EN RAGOÛT

Venison casserole

Every autumn in France some men feel the call of the wild, and from September to the New Year they gather on Sundays to walk, eat, drink, talk and sometimes they even bring home a hare, a partridge or two, or a wild duck. I am told some actually bring back wild boar and venison.

Wild venison should be hung for a few days to allow the flavour to develop and make the flesh tender. Nouvelle Cuisine chefs made it fashionable to eat venison without marinating but I think a day or two in a pungent marinade makes a more memorably-flavoured dish.

In Auvergne, where *Cantal, Bleu d'Auvergne* and *St Nectaire* cheeses mature in caves, green valleys are populated by beautiful chestnut Salers cattle and rambling streams are rich with fish, this glorious venison stew was served to me on a bleak, rainy Sunday by the Cantal Federation of Hunters. With it we ate *Truffade* (see page 176). With my version of the dish you can also serve Chestnut and Potato Purée (see page 158) or Celeriac Purée (see page 161), green lentils, noodles or potatoes and prunes cooked in red wine.

——————— *Serves 6* ———————

2¹/₄ lb (1.25 kg) boneless loin or
    shoulder of venison, cut into
    2 × 2 inch (5 × 5 cm) cubes
2 tablespoons groundnut oil
1 tablespoon plain flour
2¹/₂ tablespoons red wine vinegar
4 shallots, chopped
3 garlic cloves, chopped
3 sprigs thyme
1 bay leaf
salt and freshly ground black pepper
2 oz (50 g) unsalted butter
5 oz (150 g) smoked or unsmoked lean
    streaky bacon, diced
6 oz (175 g) whole button mushrooms

1 tablespoon chopped fresh
    flat-leaved parsley

FOR THE MARINADE
1 tablespoon vegetable oil
1 carrot, sliced
1 onion, studded with 1 clove,
    quartered
2 garlic cloves
3 shallots, halved
salt and freshly ground black pepper
1 pint (600 ml) red wine
1 teaspoon crushed coriander seeds
2 sprigs fresh thyme
1 tablespoon juniper berries, crushed
1–2 tablespoons redcurrant jelly

For the marinade, heat the oil in a saucepan or large frying-pan, add all the vegetables, sprinkle with salt, cover and cook, shaking the pan occasionally, for about 8 minutes. Add the wine, bring to the boil then lower the heat, add the coriander seeds, thyme and juniper berries, cover and simmer for 15 minutes. Leave to cool completely.

Put the venison in a large bowl, pour over the marinade, add pepper, stir to mix all the ingredients then cover and leave overnight in a cool place.

Using a slotted spoon lift the venison from the marinade and dry with paper towels. Strain the marinade and reserve everything.

Heat the oil in a large frying-pan, add the venison in batches and cook over a fairly high heat, stirring occasionally, for about 10 minutes, until evenly browned. Using a slotted spoon, transfer the venison as it is done to a heavy casserole. If necessary, add a little more oil to the frying-pan. Stir the flour into the pan and cook, stirring, until browned. Slowly pour the reserved marinade liquid and the vinegar into the frying-pan, stirring constantly, and bring to the boil. Continue to boil for 1 minute. Pour into the casserole and stir in the reserved marinade vegetables and flavourings, the fresh shallots, garlic, thyme, bay leaf, salt and pepper. Cover tightly and cook gently for $1^1/_2$–2 hours until the meat is tender. Skim and discard any fat there is on the top.

Meanwhile, heat the butter in a small frying-pan, add the bacon and sauté for 3–4 minutes. Transfer to a dish and reserve. Add the mushrooms to the pan and sauté for about 4 minutes.

Stir the mushrooms and bacon into the casserole. Stir in redcurrant jelly and salt and pepper to taste, and simmer gently for 15 minutes. Sprinkle with parsley to serve.

VEGETABLES

Les Légumes

••••••••••••••••••••••••••

RATATOUILLE

Provençal vegetable stew

The whole Mediterranean coast loves vegetables and each region in the South prepares a version of the celebrated vegetable stew *La Ratatouille*. Generally, throughout Provence the emphasis is on tomatoes, courgettes, aubergines and basil, whereas in Languedoc, mainly red, green and yellow peppers are used.

In some places, the vegetables are diced and remain firm, in others they are cooked with white wine until they all blend together; in Saint-Tropez they are sliced, layered and baked with cheese; in the Vaucluse, aubergines and tomatoes are simmered and flavoured with crushed anchovy fillets.

I have eaten puréed *Ratatouille* flavoured with a tablespoon of *Tapenade* (see page 49), and I have sampled a most refined version of this stew – a warm garlic purée in which minuscule cubes of courgettes, tomatoes, and aubergine skins (skin only!) were briefly cooked. It looked like a Seurat painting. I have heard about an interesting variation called *Bohémienne* (gypsy) where all vegetables are cut in big hunks. Why 'gypsy'? Because, supposedly, the gypsies from all over the world, who meet in the South every May, cook the dish and add to it their favourite delicacy – hedgehog!

The following recipe can be cooked until it is firm or soft, and eaten warm or cold. It may be served with poached eggs on top, it may be used as a filling for an omelette, or as an accompaniment to fish or poultry. It may also be poured over warm spaghetti or noodles with a tablespoon of olive oil, or served cold with lemon juice and olive oil drizzled over. It reheats beautifully.

Some people grill the peppers then peel them, but I find this too time consuming. I don't peel the tomatoes either; once the dish is cooked the skins are not noticeable and they do add flavour.

———— Serves 4 ————

4–5 tablespoons olive oil, or a mixture
    of olive oil and vegetable oil
2 medium onions, thinly sliced
2 red, green or yellow peppers, or a
    combination of colours, sliced
    vertically then sliced into ¹/₂ inch
    (1 cm) wide strips
2 small aubergines, sliced vertically
    then sliced into ¹/₂ inch (1 cm)
    wide strips

2 courgettes, sliced vertically then
    sliced into ¹/₂ inch (1 cm)
    wide strips
3 tomatoes, seeds removed,
    coarsely chopped
2 garlic cloves, chopped
1 tablespoon fresh thyme
1 bay leaf
salt and freshly ground black pepper
1 tablespoon chopped fresh basil
2 tablespoons chopped fresh parsley

Heat 2 tablespoons oil in a wide frying-pan and cook the onions slowly, stirring occasionally, for about 5 minutes. Add the peppers and cook for 10 minutes. Using a slotted spoon, transfer the onions and peppers to a bowl. Add a little more oil to the pan and cook the aubergines, stirring frequently, for 10 minutes. Using a slotted spoon, add to the bowl. Add the courgettes and a little more oil to the pan and cook for 2–3 minutes. Transfer to the bowl, then put a lid on top of the bowl and pour off the cooking oil.

Put the cooked vegetables in a frying-pan that is as wide and shallow as possible so water from the vegetables can evaporate easily, add the tomatoes, garlic, thyme and bay leaf, sprinkle with salt and pepper and cook over a moderate heat, stirring occasionally, for 20 minutes. If you prefer firm vegetables, sprinkle with basil and parsley, salt and pepper and serve. If you prefer a very soft *Ratatouille*, cook for a little longer. Discard excess juices and add a drizzle of olive oil just before serving.

———— **PROVENCE** ————

AUBERGINES AU COULIS DE TOMATES

Aubergines with tomato sauce

Provence shares much of the culture, climate and food of countries bordering the Mediterranean. Jenny Fajardo's Provençal version uses fresh basil. She serves the dish at room temperature as part of a summer buffet.

———————— *Serves 4* ————————

*1¹/₂ lb (750 g) aubergines, sliced
  lengthways*
salt and freshly ground black pepper
5–6 tablespoons olive oil
*6 small onions, cut lengthways into
  eight pieces*
4 garlic cloves, lightly crushed

*1 small red pepper, seeds removed,
  chopped*
*1¹/₂ lb (750 g) tomatoes, peeled, seeds
  removed, chopped*
1 bunch fresh basil
1–1¹/₂ tablespoons tomato purée

Place the aubergines in a colander and sprinkle generously with salt. Place the colander on a large plate and leave the aubergines for 30 minutes, to 'degorge'; this reduces the amount of oil the aubergines absorb when fried, and removes the bitter flavour that some large aubergines have.

Meanwhile, heat 1¹/₂ tablespoons oil in a frying pan, add the onions and garlic to the pan and cook, stirring occasionally, until softened, about 4 minutes. Add the pepper, cook for 2–3 minutes, then stir in the tomatoes and basil and leave the sauce to simmer for about 20 minutes until lightly thickened.

While the sauce is cooking, rinse the aubergines well under cold running water to remove excess salt. Pat dry with paper towels. Heat the 3–4 tablespoons oil in a large frying pan over a moderately high heat and fry the aubergine slices in batches until browned, about 7 minutes. Transfer the cooked aubergines to paper towels to drain, then lay in a serving dish.

Remove the basil from the sauce and add tomato purée and salt and pepper to taste. Pour over the aubergines. Serve warm or at room temperature.

——— **BOURBONNAIS** ———

CAROTTES VICHY

Carrots glazed with butter and sugar

The water from the springs at Vichy, in central France, has a high bicarbonate of soda content, which, when combined with the butter and parsley, give the characteristic flavour to this simple, light and delicious dish.

The carrots should be young, tender and fresh. If they are small, they can be cooked whole with their green feathery tops, if they have them, but larger ones should be cut into even-sized pieces, or sliced on the bias.

——— *Serves 4* ———

1 lb (450 g) young carrots
small pinch bicarbonate of soda
1 oz (25 g) unsalted butter

2 teaspoons caster sugar
salt
1 tablespoon chopped fresh parsley

Leave the carrots whole, cut into even-sized pieces or slice on the bias, according to their size. Put them into a heavy saucepan, just cover with water and add the bicarbonate of soda. Bring to the boil, lower the heat and simmer, shaking the pan occasionally, until the carrots are tender and nearly all the water has evaporated. Add the butter, sugar and a small pinch of salt and continue to cook, tossing the pan frequently, until the carrots are lightly glazed. Sprinkle with parsley just before serving.

Variation

In Provence, oil replaces the butter and 2 garlic cloves are added – the dish is no longer *Carottes Vichy* but it is delicious.

PURÉES DE LÉGUMES

Vegetable purées

A number of vegetable purées have been eaten for years – chestnut and cabbage purées traditionally accompany game, potato purée has been everpresent on our tables, and as a child I was given a lovely carrot and potato purée with a dribble of olive oil when I was ill. Then Nouvelle Cuisine chefs discovered that many vegetables could be turned into interesting purées. Unfortunately they overused the idea and the large Nouvelle plates looking like the palettes of abstract painters became predictable. People grew bored with their monotony and with the dearth of crunchy, fragrant food. The basic idea of turning a wide variety of vegetables into purées is, however, a good one and worth following – in moderation. As well as being delicious in themselves, vegetable purées can be used to thicken soups and sauces instead of the conventional flour or cream, giving them a lighter texture and an interesting taste.

Almost any baked, boiled or steamed vegetable – courgettes, leeks, turnips, green beans, carrots, beetroot, celeriac, cauliflower – can be transformed into a light, fluffy purée with cream, butter or olive oil. The cooked vegetables do need to be drained, though, which is why steaming is a good method to use. However, if a vegetable is too moist after it has been puréed, before adding cream, butter or olive oil, heat it gently in a saucepan, stirring until excess moisture has evaporated. Then stir in the cream, butter or olive oil. Alternatively beat in a little mashed potato, or a handful of cooked rice. You can flavour a purée with plenty of parsley, or chopped onion or garlic and some fresh herbs.

These are the vegetable purées I use the most.

CHESTNUT AND POTATO PURÉE

Traditionally served with game and pork.

——————— *Serves 4* ———————

1 lb (450 g) chestnuts
approximately 10 fl oz (300 ml) milk

1 lb (450 g) potatoes, sliced
salt and freshly ground black pepper

Cut a slash in the skin of each chestnut then cook in a saucepan of boiling water for about 5 minutes. Remove the pan from the heat. Lift a few chestnuts at a time from the water and peel off the outer skin and the thin inner one. When all the chestnuts have been peeled simmer them just covered by milk in a small saucepan for about 15–20 minutes or until tender. Meanwhile, steam the potatoes for about 6 minutes until tender then pass through a sieve into a saucepan.

Drain the chestnuts, reserving the milk. Pass the chestnuts through a coarse sieve into the pan with the potatoes. Place over a low heat and beat in the reserved milk until you have a fluffy, smooth mixture. Season with salt and pepper.

HARICOT BEAN PURÉE

Lovely with any roast beef, lamb or pork.

——————— *Serves 4* ———————

12 oz (350 g) haricot beans, soaked
*   overnight, drained*
1 onion, studded with 1 clove
2 garlic cloves
1 bay leaf
2 sprigs thyme

1 onion, chopped
1 oz (25 g) butter
2 tablespoons double cream
freshly grated nutmeg
salt and freshly ground black pepper

Put the beans in a saucepan, add the whole onion, garlic, bay leaf and thyme. Cover with cold water, boil for 10 minutes, then cover the pan and simmer for $1^1/_2$ hours until the beans are tender.

While they are cooking, cook the chopped onion in the butter, stirring occasionally, for 4–5 minutes.

Drain the beans, discard the whole onion and the herbs, then purée in a food processor or blender with the chopped onion. Transfer to a clean saucepan and reheat gently, stirring in the cream. Add nutmeg, salt and pepper to taste.

BROCCOLI PURÉE

This is very good with most meats and poultry.

——————— *Serves 4* ———————

1½ lb (750 g) broccoli
3 tablespoons double cream

salt and freshly ground black pepper

Chop the broccoli stalks then steam them with the florets for 5–8 minutes until tender. Purée in a food processor or blender then transfer to a saucepan over a low heat. Stir in the cream, and salt and pepper to taste.

FENNEL PURÉE

This is very good with any fish and with pork and game. Keep the feathery leaves from the fennel for garnish and to add flavour.

——————— *Serves 4* ———————

1¼ lb (550 g) fennel, thinly sliced
1 potato, sliced
2 tablespoons double cream or
  1 oz (25 g) butter

salt and freshly ground black pepper
1 tablespoon feathery fennel leaves, cut
  with scissors

Steam the fennel for about 10 minutes until tender. Purée in a food processor or blender then pass through a sieve into a saucepan.

Steam the potato for about 6 minutes until tender. Pass through a sieve into the pan. Heat gently and stir in the cream or butter, and salt and pepper to taste. Serve sprinkled with fennel leaves.

Opposite: BAECKEOFFE (*see page 146*).

CELERIAC PURÉE

Wonderful with pork, fish and game.

———————— *Serves 4* ————————

*1 lb (450 g) celeriac, peeled and cut
  into chunks
2 potatoes, chopped
³/₄–1 pint (450–600 ml) milk*

*3 tablespoons double cream or
  1 oz (25 g) butter
salt and freshly ground black pepper*

Put the celeriac and potatoes into a medium-sized saucepan. Add sufficient milk to just cover, cover the saucepan and simmer the vegetables for about 30 minutes until tender. Drain well then pass through a sieve into a clean saucepan. Re-heat gently, stirring with a wooden spoon to drive off excess moisture. Stir in the cream or the butter, and add salt and pepper to taste.

CABBAGE PURÉE

Delicious with pork and game.

———————— *Serves 4* ————————

*1 head white cabbage weighing about
  1¹/₂ lb (750 g)*

*1 oz (25 g) butter
salt and freshly ground black pepper*

Cut the cabbage into quarters then cut out the central core. Chop the cabbage and add to a large saucepan of boiling water. Return quickly to the boil, cover and cook for about 20 minutes. Drain. Purée the cabbage in a food processor or blender. Reheat gently in a clean saucepan then beat in the butter, and salt and pepper to taste.

Note
The vegetables can be frozen after puréeing or sieving, and preferably before the cream or butter is added. Thaw in the refrigerator then reheat gently.

Opposite: Despite the hard winters, geraniums flourish in
Alsace and can be seen throughout the region in the
summer.

PROVENCE AND LANGUEDOC

POIVRONS AUX TOMATES

Red peppers with tomatoes, herbs and garlic

Red, green and yellow peppers are readily available everywhere, but in the South of France they seem to be cooked in every possible way, yet no one ever gets tired of them.

This easy recipe is perfect as a light first course or as an accompaniment to plainly cooked meat, chicken or grilled fish.

——————— *Serves 4* ———————

2 lb (1 kg) peppers, stems removed
2 lb (1 kg) plump, firm tomatoes
3 tablespoons olive oil
3 garlic cloves, sliced

1 tablespoon fresh thyme
salt and freshly ground black pepper
2 tablespoons chopped fresh
  flat-leaved parsley

Pre-heat the oven to gas mark 6, 400°F (200°C), or pre-heat the grill.

Place the peppers on a baking sheet and put in the oven for 30 minutes, turning a couple of times, until softened. Or place them under the grill and cook, turning regularly, for about 10 minutes, until softened. Place the peppers in a large paper bag until cool enough to handle, then peel off the skins. Cut the peppers in half and discard the cores and seeds. Chop the flesh into bite-sized pieces.

Put the tomatoes in a bowl, pour over boiling water and leave for an instant. Remove the tomatoes from the water. Leave until cool enough to handle, then remove and discard the skin and seeds. Cut the tomatoes into bite-sized pieces.

Heat $2^1/_2$ tablespoons oil in a heavy-bottomed saucepan, add the garlic, sauté for 1 minute, then stir in the peppers, tomatoes and thyme. Sprinkle with salt and pepper, cover and simmer gently for 20–25 minutes, stirring from time to time. Uncover and cook a little more quickly for about 10 minutes, stirring occasionally.

Sprinkle with parsley, the remaining olive oil and freshly ground pepper before serving.

Variation

A large chopped onion, or 4 chopped anchovy fillets can be added.

*F*LANS DE *L*ÉGUMES

Vegetable Timbales

Flans de Légumes are one of the most elegant and flavourful accompaniments. Vegetables are cooked, puréed, enriched with cream and eggs, and flavoured then baked and served with fish, meat, poultry or game. In Brittany, where artichokes are so plentiful, I ate *Flan d'Artichaut*, created by Olivier Brignon, chef at the *Hôtel d'Europe* in Morlaix.

———————— *Serves 4* ————————

4 globe artichokes, total weight about 3³/₄ lb (1.6 kg)	*2 fl oz (50 ml) single cream*
juice 1 lemon	*2 eggs*
salt and freshly ground black pepper	*4 teaspoons hazelnut oil*
	cooked artichoke leaves (optional)

Snap the stems off the artichokes and discard any damaged outer leaves. Pull the outer leaves outwards from the base, then pull them downwards and off the base. Continue until you reach the pale inner leaves. Using a stainless steel knife, trim the tops of the inner leaves by one to two thirds. Rub the cut edges with lemon juice. Pare away the dark, tough exterior of the base, working in a spiral from the stem. Pull out the central, hairy 'choke' and any remaining leaves. Bring a large saucepan of water to the boil, add salt and the lemon juice, then the artichokes. Cover the pan and boil the artichokes for about 15–20 minutes until tender. Drain, rinse under cold running water and leave upside down to drain and cool.

Pre-heat the oven to gas mark 6, 400°F (200°C). Butter 4 approximately 3 inch (7.5 cm) ramekin dishes and place in a baking tin.

Break or chop the artichoke bottoms into pieces and put into the blender or food processor. Add the cream, eggs and hazelnut oil. Process briefly until smooth then season with salt and pepper.

Divide the artichoke mixture between the dishes. Pour boiling water around them to come 1 inch (2.5 cm) up the sides then cover loosely with greaseproof paper. Bake for about 30 minutes until just set in the centre. Remove the dishes from the baking tin and leave to stand for a few minutes before running the point of a knife around the edge of each dish and inverting the artichoke moulds on to a warmed plate. If liked, surround the moulds with cooked artichoke leaves.

CARROT TIMBALES

Serves 6

10 oz (300 g) carrots, chopped
1 potato, chopped
1 garlic clove
4 tablespoons chopped flat-leaved
   parsley

2 eggs
3 tablespoons single cream
pinch freshly grated nutmeg
salt and freshly ground black pepper
³/₄ oz (20 g) butter

Pre-heat the oven to gas mark 6, 400°F (200°C). Butter 6 × 3 inch (7.5 cm) ramekin dishes and place in a baking tin.

    Keeping them separate, steam the carrots and potato until tender. Put the carrots, garlic, parsley, eggs and cream into a food processor or blender and process briefly to mix. Pass the potato through a sieve into a bowl then stir in the carrot mixture. Add freshly grated nutmeg and salt and pepper to taste. Divide between the dishes, then pour boiling water around them to come 1 inch (2.5 cm) up the sides. Cover the dishes with greaseproof paper and cook for about 30 minutes until lightly set in the centre. Leave to stand for a few minutes before unmoulding. Place a small knob of butter on each before serving.

GARLIC TIMBALES

Lovely with lamb and pork.

Serves 4

approximately 18 garlic cloves
5 fl oz (150 ml) single cream
2 eggs

salt and freshly ground black pepper
¹/₂ oz (15 g) unsalted butter

Pre-heat the oven to gas mark 6, 400°F (200°C). Butter 4 × 2¹/₂ inch (6 cm) ramekin dishes and place in a baking tin.

    Boil the garlic cloves for about 3 minutes. Drain well then put into a blender or food processor. Add the cream, eggs and seasoning and mix together. Divide between the ramekins then pour boiling water around them to come 1 inch (2.5 cm) up the sides. Cover the dishes with foil and bake for 15–20 minutes until lightly set in the centre. Leave to stand for a few minutes before unmoulding. Place a small knob of butter on each before serving.

Spinach Timbales

These go well with veal, poultry or lamb.

———————— *Serves 6* ————————

*1¹/₂ lb (750 g) fresh spinach, or 10 oz
(300 g) frozen spinach, thawed and
well drained
2 oz (50 g) butter
1 whole egg*

*1 egg yolk
2 fl oz (50 ml) double cream
freshly grated nutmeg
salt and freshly ground black pepper*

Pre-heat the oven to gas mark 6, 400°F (200°C). Butter 6 × 3 inch (7.5 cm) ramekin dishes and place in a baking tin.

If using fresh spinach, wash the leaves, shake off excess moisture but do not dry them, then place in a saucepan. Cover and place over a fairly high heat, shaking the pan occasionally until the leaves start to wilt. Stir the spinach, cover again and continue to cook until the spinach is completely wilted and tender. Tip fresh or frozen spinach into a food processor or blender and process until smooth. Return to the pan, add 1¹/₂ oz (40 g) butter and cook until all the excess moisture has evaporated. Remove from the heat and beat in the egg, egg yolk and cream. Add freshly grated nutmeg and salt and pepper to taste. Divide the spinach mixture between the dishes and then pour boiling water around them. Cover the dishes with greaseproof paper and cook for 23–25 minutes until lightly set in the centre. Allow to stand for a few minutes before unmoulding. Place a dot of butter on each timbale before serving.

Note

To reheat timbales place in a warm oven for 5 minutes before un-moulding.

*A*RTICHAUTS À LA *B*ARIGOULE

Braised stuffed artichokes

In Provence, small purple artichokes are eaten raw and cooked, warm and cold, but this is my favourite recipe. It is a tasty, light dish that is perfect for a simple lunch, or a first course for a more substantial meal.

———— *Serves 4* ————

8 small purple artichokes, or 4 small globe artichokes
juice ¹/₂ lemon
4 tablespoons olive oil
2 onions, chopped
4 tablespoons chopped fresh parsley
2 slices lean streaky bacon, chopped

2 garlic cloves, crushed
salt and freshly ground black pepper
2 carrots, sliced
3 garlic cloves, unpeeled
1 bay leaf
1 sprig thyme
4 fl oz (120 ml) dry white wine
4 fl oz (120 ml) water

Snap the stems from the artichokes, and remove the tough outer leaves. Cut off the hard tips of the remaining leaves with strong kitchen scissors. If using globe artichokes, place them stalk-ends down in a large saucepan of salted, boiling water to which the lemon juice has been added, and boil for 5 minutes. Remove the artichokes from the water and place upside-down to drain.

Using a small spoon or a melon baller, remove the fuzzy choke from the centre of each artichoke, scraping the bottom vigorously to clean it as thoroughly as possible.

Heat 2 tablespoons olive oil in a large frying-pan and gently cook a third of the onions for about 5 minutes, stirring occasionally. Remove from the heat and stir in the parsley, bacon, crushed garlic and salt and pepper.

Place the artichokes upside-down and press down with your fist to force the leaves apart. Divide onion mixture between the artichokes.

Place the carrots, remaining onions, the garlic cloves, and remaining olive oil in a heavy-bottomed saucepan or casserole which the artichokes will just fit in a single layer. Place the artichokes upright on the vegetables and sprinkle with salt and pepper. Add the bay leaf and sprig of thyme, and cook over a moderate heat for 5–10 minutes. Add the wine, bring to the boil, then simmer for 3–5 minutes. Add the water, cover and simmer gently for 45 minutes until the artichokes are tender. Check to see whether you need to add a little more water. Place the artichokes in a warm shallow serving dish, cover and keep warm. Using a large spoon, force the carrots, onions and garlic through a sieve placed over the saucepan or casserole. Stir the purée back into the cooking juices and simmer for 3–5 minutes. Discard the bay leaf and sprig of thyme and pour over the artichokes. Serve at once.

PROVENCE AND LANGUEDOC

GRATIN DE COURGETTES

Courgette, rice, onion and cheese casserole

In summer when the tomatoes are firm and fleshy I place four tomato halves, cut side up and the seeds removed, on the courgettes, before sprinkling over the breadcrumbs. I serve as a first course, or as an accompaniment to roast meat or poultry.

As a variation you can purée the vegetables with the rice and eggs then bake for 20–25 minutes.

Serves 4

*2 × ¹/₂ inch (1 cm) thick slices lean,
    streaky bacon, finely diced*
3 tablespoons olive oil
3 onions, thinly sliced
6 courgettes, diced
2¹/₂ oz (65 g) cooked rice
*3 oz (75 g) Gruyère or Parmesan
    cheese, grated*

*6 tablespoons chopped, fresh
    flat-leaved parsley*
2 eggs, beaten
1 tablespoon fresh thyme
salt and freshly ground black pepper
4 tablespoons fresh breadcrumbs

Pre-heat the oven to gas mark 5, 375°F (190°C). Oil a gratin dish.

Gently cook the bacon in a large frying-pan for a few minutes, add 2 tablespoons oil, then the onions, and cook, stirring occasionally, for about 4 minutes. Stir in the courgettes and cook over a low heat for 15 minutes, stirring from time to time.

Remove the pan from the heat and stir in the rice, cheese, parsley, eggs, thyme, and salt and pepper. Transfer to the dish, sprinkle with the breadcrumbs and drizzle over the remaining olive oil. Bake for 15 minutes until the top is crisp and golden.

CÈPES SAUTÉS

Sautéed ceps

Ceps can be very expensive, unless you've found them yourself, but this recipe is not really worth trying with ordinary field mushrooms.

When I was visiting the Comte and Comtesse Manoir de Juaye at their home, Château de Brie, in Limousin, some of their neighbours brought them the first ceps of the season. When sautéeing ceps the comtesse used lard instead of vegetable oil and butter, and sautéd 3 sliced garlic cloves before adding the ceps caps and stems; she omitted the shallots. Madame la Comtesse, being an enthusiastic cook, also showed me how she preserves ceps for the winter. She makes the following recipe, minus the lemon juice, then packs the ceps into sterilised jars, which are tightly sealed before being cooked in simmering water for an hour.

Ceps should be covered with an even, deep-brown skin and be very firm and fresh. The best ones are medium-sized. Ceps are delicious stuffed, in omelettes and casseroles, or simply sautéed in butter.

——— *Serves 6* ———

2 lb (1 kg) very firm ceps
2–3 tablespoons vegetable oil
about 1 oz (25 g) butter
salt and freshly ground black pepper

2 shallots, finely chopped
juice ½ lemon
2 tablespoons freshly chopped parsley

Do not wash the ceps – just wipe them dry with a damp cloth. Separate the stems from the caps. Keep only 1 inch (2.5 cm) of the stems and discard the rest. Cut the caps into ½ inch (1 cm) thick slices, and chop the reserved stems. Heat the oil in a deep frying-pan. When it is very hot, add the butter, wait for 1 minute, then add the sliced ceps and sprinkle with salt and pepper. Toss with a wooden spoon, then cook for about 4 minutes until golden. Lower the heat, cook for a further 5 minutes then increase the heat for 2 more minutes. Using a slotted spoon, transfer the ceps to a warmed serving dish and keep warm.

Add more butter and oil if necessary. Add the shallots and chopped ceps stems and sauté until golden. Add to the ceps caps, sprinkle with seasoning, lemon juice and parsley and serve on warm plates.

ARDENNES

*E*NDIVES *G*RATINÉES

Chicory with cheese and ham

In England, what you refer to as chicory, we, in France, call *endives*. To confuse things further when I refer to a curly, green-leaved type of lettuce, I say '*chicorée*' and you say '*endive*'. However, cooking is not about trying to clarify the oddities of language. It is about treating ingredients sympathetically so they become delicious dishes. Choose small or medium-sized chicory that is creamy white and closed at the tip.

Chicory is often boiled, drained, wrapped in a slice of ham, covered with a cheese sauce, and then baked until crisp, but I prefer this recipe as it is lighter. There is no heavy sauce, the chicory is lightly caramelised, which softens its bitter taste, and the ham and cheese are more of an accent. Serve with chicken, roast pork or grilled lamb chops.

Serves 4

8 chicory heads	*1¹/₂ oz (40 g) unsalted butter, diced*
salt and freshly ground black pepper	*4 oz (100 g) cooked ham, finely*
4 tablespoons water	*chopped*
juice 1 lemon	*1¹/₂ oz (40 g) Gruyère cheese, grated*
	pinch grated nutmeg

With a sharp knife, cut each head of chicory in half lengthways. Place the chicory, head to tail, in a single layer in a large, heavy-bottomed frying-pan. Sprinkle with salt, add the water and lemon juice, cover and bring to the boil. Simmer gently for 15 minutes.

Pre-heat the oven to gas mark 7, 425°F (220°C). Butter a shallow ovenproof dish that is large enough to hold the chicory in a single layer.

Using a fish slice, transfer the chicory to the dish. Dot the butter over the top and bake for about 25 minutes, basting a couple of times, until browned. Sprinkle the ham, cheese, nutmeg and a little pepper over the top and return to the oven for about 5 minutes.

GRATIN DE TOMATES, COURGETTES ET ONIONS

Tomato, courgette and onion gratin

This dish is light, flavourful, inexpensive and may be prepared and left to cook while you sit and chat. When you are ready, you just have to take the crisp gratin from the oven or let it rest in the cooling oven for a while.

The vegetables should be fresh; the courgettes should be firm and shiny, and the tomatoes should be plump and heavy. For the most flavourful gratin, the olive oil should be 'virgin', fruity and fresh.

Serves 4

4 tablespoons olive oil
2 large onions, thinly sliced
3 garlic cloves, sliced
1¹/₂ lb (750 g) courgettes, thickly sliced
1¹/₂ lb (750 g) firm, plump tomatoes, skinned, seeds removed, sliced
3 bay leaves

1¹/₂ tablespoons chopped fresh thyme
4 tablespoons chopped fresh parsley, or basil
salt and freshly ground black pepper
1 oz (25 g) Gruyère or Parmesan cheese, grated
1 tablespoon fresh breadcrumbs

Pre-heat the oven to gas mark 5, 375°F (190°C). Oil a baking dish.

Heat 1¹/₂ tablespoons oil in a frying-pan and sauté the onions for 5 minutes. Add the garlic, cook for 1–2 minutes, then add a little more oil and the courgettes. Sauté for 3 minutes, then add the tomatoes and cook for 5 minutes.

Layer the vegetables in the dish with the bay leaves, thyme, parsley or basil, and salt and pepper.

Mix together the cheese and breadcrumbs. Sprinkle evenly over the top of the vegetables, drizzle a little olive oil all over and bake for 15–20 minutes, until crisp and lightly browned. Serve warm or lukewarm.

GRATIN DE POMMES DE TERRE

Potatoes baked with milk or cream, and cheese

The subject of potato gratins raises many questions and remains a cause of hot debate. Should cream or milk be used? Or broth, as is used when making *Gratin Savoyard*? Should an egg be added? Should the potatoes be cooked in milk first then baked with cheese and cream?

It is fool-hardy to claim to provide a final, or definitive recipe but the following, which has been adapted and tested over the years, is, for me, the ultimate potato gratin. In its simplicity it has every virtue. It is easy to prepare, creamy inside, crisp outside. It can be inexpensive (I often replace cream or milk with undiluted, unsweetened evaporated milk), and it is versatile. I serve it with roast chicken, lamb or pork, fish baked with lemon and tomatoes, and a selection of cold meats and charcuterie. I also serve it with a tossed green salad for a simple lunch.

A potato gratin seems to be appropriate for almost any occasion, from a buffet for 30 people, to a small, quiet, just-family dinner in the kitchen, to a light-and-simple lunch for visiting friends.

——————— *Serves 4–6* ———————

2 cloves garlic, crushed
2 oz (50 g) unsalted butter
1¹/₂ lb (750 g) potatoes, thinly sliced
4 shallots, chopped
salt and white pepper

freshly grated nutmeg
4 oz (100 g) Gruyère cheese, grated
15 fl oz (450 ml) single cream, milk,
    or evaporated milk

Pre-heat the oven to gas mark 4, 350°F (180°C).

Rub a large ovenproof dish with 1 of the garlic cloves then spread half of the butter over the inside of the dish. Layer the potatoes, shallots, salt, pepper, nutmeg, the remaining garlic clove, and two-thirds of the cheese in the dish.

Bring the cream, milk or evaporated milk to the boil and slowly pour over the potato mixture, allowing it to trickle through the layers. Sprinkle over the remaining cheese, dot with the remaining butter, cover lightly with a piece of lightly oiled foil and bake for 1 hour. Remove the foil and bake for a further 20 minutes until the inside is creamy and the top very crisp.

GALETTES DE POMMES DE TERRE

Crisp potato, onion and herb cakes

What a joy to walk in Strasbourg with its decorated timber houses, cobbled streets, carved wooden balconies and numerous canals and rivers with their pretty covered bridges and watch the storks in their huge nests in the park. All this is seductive enough for a while, then one suddenly realises that the key to the city's life is elsewhere – in the *winstubs*. A *winstub* is a sort of Alsatian bistro-café-inn where animated conversations, good food and energy prevail. Whether they have a plump porcelain stove, a brass grandfather clock and old beams, or a plainer setting, they are always cosy and lively, and consistently serve a rich variety of Alsace specialities along with Alsace wines and schnaps. Traditionally neither coffee nor beer are served. Marie-Claude Piéton and Thérèse Willer took me for a splendid luncheon in the *winstub Au Pont du Corbeau*. We ate stuffed calves' hearts with red cabbage sautéed with onions, apples and chestnuts, and boiled beef with raw vegetables. But mostly we ate my favourite Alsatian dish, *galettes de pommes de terre*, golden, crisp and irresistibly inviting potato cakes served with a bowl of fresh curd cheese and a crisp green salad. *Galettes* may be served as a light lunch dish or as an accompaniment to roast lamb or pork, or grilled steak. A dilemma: I have been unable to decide which of my two *galette* recipes I should choose for this book so I offer both. I am so taken by them I am tempted to serve them both to my potato-loving friends.

RECIPE *I*

This recipe makes one large, baked galette flavoured with bacon

Serves 4

1¼ lb (550 g) potatoes, peeled and
 thickly sliced
1 tablespoon groundnut oil
8 oz (225 g) lean streaky bacon,
 finely chopped
2 onions, chopped

2 teaspoons fresh thyme
salt and white pepper
1 oz (25 g) unsalted butter
1 tablespoon finely chopped fresh
 chervil, parsley or chives

Pre-heat the oven to gas mark 4, 350°F (180°C). Grease an ovenproof dish.

Put the potatoes into a bowl. Heat the oil in a thick frying pan, add the bacon and cook, stirring occasionally, for 2–3 minutes. Using a slotted spoon, transfer to the bowl with the potatoes. Add the onions to the pan, cook for 3–4 minutes, stirring from time to time, until beginning to colour and soften. Pour into the bowl with the thyme and salt and pepper. Toss all the ingredients together to coat the potatoes.

Transfer to the dish, press down hard on the top of the mixture with a fish slice then dot with the butter and bake for 30 minutes. Press firmly on the potatoes and cook for a further 30 minutes, pressing on the potatoes a couple of times more.

Run a knife around the inside edge of the potatoes to loosen, place a warmed plate on top, and unmould on a warm round serving dish. Sprinkle with chervil, parsley or chives.

RECIPE *II*

This makes thin galettes that are like potato pancakes. They are served with a selection of accompaniments – soft, cream cheese, very finely sliced onions and horseradish. Potatoes that are boiled before being fried remain much more crisp than if fried from raw.

———————— *Serves 4* ————————

*1¹/₄ lb (550 g) small–medium sized
    potatoes*
2 eggs, lightly beaten
1 onion, very finely chopped
*2 teaspoons finely chopped, fresh
    flat-leaved parsley*
1 teaspoon finely chopped fresh chives
pinch freshly grated nutmeg
salt and freshly ground black pepper

2 tablespoons groundnut oil
¹/₂ oz (15 g) butter

TO SERVE
*curd cheese or a mixture of soured
    cream and drained, sieved
    cottage cheese*
thinly sliced onions
horseradish sauce

Boil the potatoes for about 15 minutes until cooked but firm. Drain well, leave until they are cool enough to handle then grate them on a medium size grater into a bowl. Add the eggs, onion, herbs, nutmeg, salt, and pepper and stir thoroughly.

Heat the oil and the butter in a heavy-bottomed frying-pan, spoon in half of the potato mixture to make a thin layer, press down then cook over a moderate heat for about 4 minutes on each side, turning over half-way through with a fish slice. Transfer to a warm plate and keep warm while frying the remaining mixture in the same way.

Sprinkle the *galettes* with pepper and serve piping hot with curd cheese, or soured cream mixed with drained, sieved cottage cheese, thinly sliced onions and horseradish sauce.

— **THROUGHOUT FRANCE** —

POMMES FRITES

Potato chips

The French love sophisticated vegetables such as artichokes and asparagus, but when it comes to basic crowd-pleasing food, *frites*, potato chips, dry and crisp outside, soft inside and crunchy with salt, remain everyone's favourite. Whether they are cooked in lard, beef or goose-fat, groundnut or corn oil, whether they are cut into matchsticks, thicker *Pont Neuf*, traditional chips, or thin, round slices, a pile of piping-hot *frites* sprinkled around a roast chicken or a steak spells immediate carefree pleasure. Of course, anyone can serve soggy, pale, greasy chips, but perfect ones require a little knowledge. You have to use a firm, mature maincrop variety of potato, such as King Edward, Désirée or Maris Piper, and an oil that can be heated to a high temperature without burning – groundnut oil is the best, but you can also use sunflower or corn oil. The oil must be at the correct temperature when the potatoes are added, so a cooking thermometer is useful. If you do not have one, test the heat of the oil by dropping in a cube of bread: when it turns golden brown in 1 minute, the oil is ready.

————————— *Serves 6* —————————

2 lb (1 kg) firm potatoes　　　　　　*salt and freshly ground black pepper*
groundnut or corn oil

Peel, slice and cut the potatoes into sticks, keeping them all to the same size and shape. Leave them in a bowl of cold water for 30 minutes then dry them thoroughly with paper towels. Keep them wrapped until ready to use so they will not discolour.

Add sufficient oil to a deep-fat fryer so that it is only one-third full to avoid the danger of the oil frothing over when the chips are added. Heat the oil to 350°F (180°C). Using the chip basket lower the chips into the hot oil and raise the heat a little so the temperature will not be lowered too much. Shake the pan gently for a few minutes to let the moisture evaporate. After 6 minutes or so the chips will rise to the surface and float. Lift them from the pan in the chip basket and let them drain and cool for about 5 minutes.

Re-heat the oil to 375°F (190°C). Lower the chips into it when it is the correct temperature and cook for 1 or 2 minutes, so they will become crisp and golden.

Lift the chips out of the oil and scatter them on a dish lined with paper towels. Shake a little and discard the greasy papers. Sprinkle lightly with salt, toss and serve. Never cover potato chips as they will become soggy.

Variation

I sprinkle freshly ground pepper, a little crushed garlic and chopped parsley or fresh thyme on top of my *frites*, but that is the Provençal in me.

TRUFFADE

Mashed potato with cheese

Truffade comes from the hilly pastures of Auvergne, in the centre of France, where so many splendid cheeses are prepared.

After Monsieur Morin had spent a morning explaining to me about *Bleu d'Auvergne*, mellow *Saint Nectaire* and mature *Cantal* in his cold, humid cheese cellar in Aurillac, he invited me to his warm kitchen to taste a warming dish of potatoes beaten with cheese, which he called *Truffade*. Other versions of *Truffade* are made by adding cheese to a 'cake' of fried potato and bacon.

In Auvergne *Truffade* is prepared with fresh *tome*, but in Britain a combination of white Cheshire cheese and soured cream will produce an acceptable alternative as regards flavour, but the mixture will not form the 'strings' that occur when *tome* is used. Serve with either a green tossed salad, or with a roast meat.

Serves 6

2 tablespoons pork fat or vegetable oil	*6 fl oz (175 ml) soured cream*
2 lb (1 kg) potatoes, sliced	*salt and freshly ground black pepper*
12 oz (350 g) white Cheshire cheese,	*1–2 cloves garlic, crushed*
cut into very thin slices, or crumbled	*2 tablespoons finely chopped parsley*

Heat the oil in a large heavy-bottomed frying pan and, when it is hot, add the potatoes and cook, covered, for about 25 minutes, stirring from time to time with a wooden spoon. Some potatoes will be soft, some will remain crisp.

Sprinkle with pepper and a little salt, cover briefly then remove from the heat and add the cheese. Cover again for a minute or so, then add the cream and beat well with a wooden spoon, lifting the mixture slightly. Add the garlic and parsley before serving.

Opposite: GRATIN DE TOMATES, COURGETTES ET ONIONS (*see page 170*).

-------- VENDÉE --------

MOJETTES AU JAMBON

Haricot beans with ham and tomatoes

Mojettes are a staple of the Vendée, once one of the poorest areas in France. Madame Gardot prepared them for us and her family for a weekday lunch, serving them in the traditional, regional way with slices of local ham sautéed in butter to remove some of the salt. To serve the beans as an accompaniment to a main course, omit the bacon and ham.

-------- *Serves 4* --------

12 oz (350 g) white haricot beans,	*4 oz (100 g) streaky bacon, diced*
soaked overnight, drained and rinsed	*4 oz (100 g) ham, diced*
1 onion studded with 1 clove	*4 tomatoes, skinned, seeds*
2 carrots, sliced	*removed, quartered*
2 bay leaves	*2 garlic cloves, crushed*
2 tablespoons vegetable oil, or 1 oz	*small bunch fresh thyme*
(25 g) margarine	*salt and freshly ground black pepper*
4 shallots, sliced	*1 tablespoon chopped fresh chives*
	or parsley

Put the beans in a saucepan, add the whole onion, carrots and bay leaves, cover with water, bring to the boil, boil for 10 minutes then cover and simmer for about 1¹/₂ hours until tender. The beans must remain covered with water as they cook, so add some more if necessary.

Meanwhile, heat the oil or margarine in a frying-pan, add the shallots and sauté for about 4 minutes until soft, stirring occasionally. Add the bacon and ham and cook for 5 minutes, stirring from time to time. Stir in the tomatoes, garlic and thyme, and cook for 5 minutes.

Drain the beans well, discard the whole onion and bay leaves then stir into the frying-pan. Simmer together for 20 minutes. Season with salt and pepper then sprinkle over the chives or parsley.

Opposite: GALETTES DE POMMES DE TERRE served with cream cheese and onions (*see page 172*).

CHOU FARCI

Stuffed cabbage

For *Chou farci* the cabbage must be a dark green, thick-leaved Savoy, and the stuffing must contain pork in some form. Otherwise it's all according to tradition and personal choice.

Chou farci is a hearty, warming dish and ideal for cold winter nights and large appetites. It is also a good way of transforming left-over ham or roast pork into a glorious creation. You may like to prepare the cabbage ahead of time. If so stuff and tie it into a ball, then cover and refrigerate it until 1 hour before you want to cook it. Leave the cabbage at room temperature for 1 hour then proceed with the recipe.

——————— *Serves 6* ———————

1 Savoy cabbage, weighing about
   2¹/₄ lb (1.25 g)
1 oz (25 g) butter
1 tablespoon vegetable oil
1 large onion, coarsely chopped
6 oz (175 g) smoked lean streaky
   bacon, cut into ¹/₄ inch (6 mm) cubes
10 oz (300 g) cooked well-flavoured
   ham, chopped
3 cloves garlic, finely chopped
2 eggs, lightly beaten
3 oz (75 g) rice, cooked and drained
8 tablespoons chopped fresh parsley
1¹/₂ teaspoons freshly ground coriander
salt and freshly ground black pepper

FOR THE VEGETABLES
Choose as many as you wish.

2 long stalks celery, cut into 2 inch
   (5 cm) lengths
2 courgettes, sliced lengthways and cut
   into 2 inch (5 cm) pieces

2 fennel bulbs, halved lengthways
2–4 small turnips, depending on size,
   halved or quartered
2 carrots, halved lengthways, then cut
   into 2 inch (5 cm) long pieces
2 large, fresh garlicky or very spicy
   sausages, pricked with a fork
   before cooking

FOR THE SAUCE
6 fl oz (175 ml) olive oil
salt and freshly ground black pepper
1 teaspoon freshly ground coriander
1 tablespoon chopped mixed fresh herbs
   such as thyme, majoram, chervil
   and parsley
2 large tomatoes, skinned, seeds
   removed, diced

TO GARNISH
chopped fresh herbs such as parsley,
   chives and tarragon

With a sharp knife, cut out most of the core of the cabbage and discard any straggly leaves. Bring a large saucepan of water to the boil, lower in the cabbage, stalk-end down, and boil for 10–15 minutes. Transfer the cabbage to a colander and refresh under cold, running water. When cool, peel off the leaves, cut away the coarse central veins from the outer leaves then drain the leaves on paper towels. Finely chop and reserve the heart.

Heat the butter and oil in a large frying-pan. Add the onion and cook, stirring occasionally for about 4 minutes, until soft. Add the bacon and cook for a further 5 minutes, stirring from time to time. Transfer to a large bowl then stir in the chopped cabbage heart, ham, garlic, eggs, rice, parsley, coriander and pepper. The stuffing should be rather coarse.

Line a bowl with a large piece of muslin, cheesecloth or a thin tea towel. Lay a few cabbage leaves on the cloth, overlapping them slightly so they line the bowl. (You may like to place a few thin slices of bacon on the cloth before adding the first layer of cabbage leaves.) Sprinkle the leaves with salt and pepper, then spread on a thin layer of stuffing. Cover with 2 or 3 cabbage leaves, another layer of stuffing and so on until you have used all the ingredients, except 2 cabbage leaves. Use these for a final covering. Gather up the edges of the cloth and tie together with string to make a neat ball.

Half-fill a large saucepan with water, add salt and bring to the boil. Place the stuffed cabbage in the boiling water, add more boiling water, if necessary, to cover the cabbage, lower the heat and simmer for $1^1/_4$–$1^1/_2$ hours. Add the vegetables and sausages and simmer for a further 30 minutes, until the vegetables are tender. Alternatively, the vegetables and sausages can be steamed in a basket, over the cabbage.

Meanwhile, prepare the sauce by mixing the olive oil, salt, pepper, coriander and herbs together in a bowl until thoroughly combined, then stir in the tomatoes. Stir again before serving.

Lift the cabbage from the saucepan and place in a colander. Cut open the string with scissors, loosen the cloth and carefully slip it from under the cabbage. Place a large, warm serving plate over the top of the colander and, holding on tight to the plate and colander, turn them together in a decisive gesture. Remove the colander. Sprinkle the cabbage with some of the chopped fresh herbs. Lift the sausages to a warm plate and slice them. Add the vegetables to the plate. Pour about $^1/_2$ pint (300 ml) of the hot cooking broth in a warm serving bowl and sprinkle over the remaining fresh herbs. Take the cabbage, the vegetables and sausages and the bowls of sauce and broth to the table and serve at once.

CRÊPES AND GALETTES

Breton pancakes

Ignited with a flourish by waiters in restaurants or bathed with orange butter, *crêpes* have now become a great culinary spectacle, but they used to be a simple, staple food of Breton farmers and fishermen, and were eaten in the same way as bread. Originally they were made with buckwheat and called *galettes*, but, after wheat was introduced to the area, wheat flour was used for *galettes* for the sick and rich people as it makes the mixture lighter. Nowadays, these are generally called *crêpes* and will have a sweet filling whereas buckwheat *galettes*, being heavier, are usually savoury. But beware, the definitions can vary from one part of Brittany to another, and outside the region the word *crêpe* is often used for both sweet and savoury pancakes. They are served at Candlemas, for dessert or as a base for left-overs.

In Pont l'Abbé, I spent a morning at the *Hôtel Bretagne* with Madame Josette Cossec, who makes about 1,600 *galettes* and *crêpes* a day. I watched her beat the batter, spread it over the *galettière*, special griddle, with a deft movement of the special wooden spatula, flip it over then top it with beaten egg. As she worked she told me how she used to spend her Fridays with Granny, each child preparing a pile of *galettes*, and explained how the first is always for the dog (too thick and too pasty), the second always offered to the farm-hands (out of courtesy), how *crêpes* and *galettes* wrapped in fine fabric were added to a soldier's pack, or taken on religious processions as a snack, how some were kept to be dried on a string stretched across the room as they were made, how buckwheat makes a soft *galette* and wheat a more crisp one, and how buckwheat *galettes* can be made with just plenty of beating and no eggs if you are skilful enough. As I was too busy tasting I didn't have any questions to ask nor response to make except a satisfied purring.

GALETTES

Serves 4–6

5 oz (150 g) wheat flour	*2 eggs*
4 oz (100 g) buckwheat flour	*16 fl oz (475 ml) water*
1 teaspoon salt	*butter, for frying*

Stir the flours and salt together in a bowl, and form a well in the centre. Pour the eggs into the well then, stirring with a wooden spoon, slowly pour in the water until the mixture feels like a creamy custard. Beat for about 10 minutes to incorporate air bubbles that will allow the batter to absorb butter as it cooks, moistening it and making it tastier.

Melt a small knob of butter in a frying-pan. Swirl it around to cover the bottom of the pan then pour it out. Add 2 or 3 tablespoons of the batter to the pan, swirl it around to cover the base in a thin layer then cook over a fairly high heat until set and light brown underneath. Turn over and brown on the other side. Add a little more butter to the pan and continue making more *galettes* until all the batter has been used.

For the Fillings

Galettes were originally spread with lightly salted butter and folded in four but nowadays the range of fillings is staggering.

- Coarsely chopped onions sautéed in butter.
- Chopped and sautéed slivers of ham or bacon.
- Finely chopped parsley, chervil, chives, shallot and garlic stirred into softened butter with a little pepper.
- An egg broken into the centre of the *galette*, sprinkled with salt, pepper and dotted with butter.
- Chopped fried sausages mixed with diced cooked apples.
- Chopped tomatoes and onions cooked with a little thyme, then chives or parsley sprinkled over the folded *galette*.
- Finely chopped bacon, tomatoes, onions and parsley cooked slowly in butter, then a little cider added.
- 'Johnny' – sautéed chopped onions, mixed with a little dry white wine, salt and pepper, then topped with a knob of butter after placing on the *galette*. (These are named after the men who went to England to sell onions which they hung round their necks and from their bicycles.)
- Grated or sliced cheese with a little butter or herb butter on the top.
- Skinned sardine fillets, with a knob of butter placed on the folded *galette*. Wait for a second before serving.
- Skinned smoked trout fillets with a little butter and herbs.
- Seafood such as mussels, cockles, prawns and scallops, plus their cooking liquid and a drop of brandy spooned over.
- Fish topped with sautéed shallots, parsley and nutmeg, covered with light tomato sauce and a little white wine and baked.

You can also try, scrambled eggs, sausages and smoked salmon.

CRÊPES

——— *Makes about 12 crêpes* ———

4 oz (100 g) wheat flour
2 small eggs, beaten
1 tablespoon sugar (optional)
10 fl oz (300 ml) light-flavoured beer,
  milk or water
1 tablespoon melted butter or
  vegetable oil
2 tablespoons orange flower water, or
  brandy (optional)
1 teaspoon salt

FOR THE FILLINGS
jam
honey and lemon juice
cooked sliced pears, spread on butter
grated plain chocolate, or cocoa powder
sliced apples marinated in lemon juice
  and sugar, then baked. You can also
  sprinkle Calvados or Benedictine
  over just before serving piping hot

Put the flour into a bowl. Make a well in the centre, add the eggs, and sugar, if using, and beat well. Add the beer, milk or water then the butter or oil, the orange flower water or brandy, if using, and salt. Allow the mixture to rest.

After 1 hour stir again: there should be no lumps and the batter will be perfectly smooth.

Add a small knob of butter to a hot frying-pan. Pour about 3 tablespoons batter into the pan then tilt in all directions so that the batter runs in a thin film over the surface. Pour off any excess batter into a bowl. After a minute or so, the sides of the *crêpe* will separate from the sides of the pan. Shake the pan. Lift the edge of the *crêpe* with a spatula and turn, or toss it in the air. Brown the other side for a few seconds then slide the *crêpe* onto a plate placed over hot water. Add a little oil or butter to the pan and continue to make more *crêpes* until all the batter has been used.

Note

If you don't have friends and children around you in the kitchen eagerly waiting to take each *crêpe* as it comes from the pan, you can keep the *crêpes* warm by stacking them on a plate placed over a saucepan of simmering water.

DESSERTS

Les Desserts

•••••••••••••••••••••••••••••••••

MOUSSE AU CHOCOLAT

Chocolate mousse flavoured with coffee and orange

Chocolate Mousse is a must in any cook's repertoire, as it is easy to make and always popular with everyone. Serve with thin biscuits, sliced oranges and sliced grapefruit sprinkled with honey, vanilla-flavoured custard, or whipped cream mixed with a little soured cream.

——————— *Serves 6–8* ———————

6 oz (175 g) plain chocolate, chopped
¹/₂ oz (15 g) unsalted butter
2 tablespoons instant coffee powder
4 eggs, separated
1¹/₂ oz (40 g) caster sugar
2–3 teaspoons grated orange rind
1 tablespoon finely chopped candied
   orange peel (optional)

2 tablespoons Grand Marnier
   or Cointreau
3 tablespoons whipping cream, chilled
1 egg white

TO DECORATE
grated plain chocolate, or
   cocoa powder

Place the chocolate, butter and coffee powder in a bowl, place over a saucepan of hot, not boiling, water and leave until the chocolate has melted, stirring occasionally. Remove the bowl from the saucepan and leave to cool.

Meanwhile, whisk the egg yolks with 1 tablespoon sugar until thick and pale yellow. Using a tablespoon, stir in the chocolate and coffee mixture, the orange rind and peel, if using, and the Grand Marnier or Cointreau.

Lightly whip the cream and fold into the chocolate mixture. Whisk all the egg whites until stiff but not dry, then gradually whisk in the remaining sugar. Using a large metal spoon, gently fold into the chocolate mixture in 3 or 4 batches. Pour into a large pretty serving bowl or individual dishes. Cover and place in the refrigerator for 2–3 hours.

Decorate the top with grated plain chocolate or sieved cocoa powder, before serving.

Variation

The mousse can also be served frozen. Pour the prepared mixture into a lightly oiled charlotte mould, or similar freezer-proof mould, tin or dish. Cover with foil and freeze for 24 hours. To unmould, dip the bottom of the mould, tin or dish into a bowl of hot water for a few seconds, place a large serving plate over the mould, tin or dish and, holding tightly to the side of the mould and the edge of the plate, turn them over in a decisive movement and give a sharp shake. Sprinkle the grated chocolate or cocoa powder over the top and serve.

ALSACE

*M*OUSSE AU *K*IRSCH

Kirsch mousse

René de Miscault produces a wide variety of eaux-de-vie, some made from wild berries of the Vosges mountains, others from more exotic ingredients, such as fresh ginger. But France's most popular eau-de-vie is cherry flavoured kirsch, which Madame de Miscault uses in this very rich but easy dessert.

Serves 4

5 egg yolks
5 oz (150 g) caster sugar
5–6 tablespoons kirsch
8 fl oz (250 ml) crème fraîche, or
    whipping cream

FOR THE GARNISH (optional)
cherries marinated in kirsch

Using a wooden spatula, beat the egg yolks with the sugar in a bowl placed over a saucepan of hot, but not boiling, water until thick and light, about 10 minutes.

Remove the bowl from the heat, stir in the kirsch and continue to beat until the mixture is cold.

In a separate bowl, beat the crème fraîche or cream until soft peaks form, then, using a large metal spoon, gently fold into the egg yolk mixture. Pour into individual glasses and chill for a few hours. Serve garnished with cherries marinated in kirsch, if liked.

GÂTEAU AUX MARRONS

Chestnut, chocolate and brandy cake

This recipe is indispensable in more ways than one: it is easy to remember as the proportions of the main ingredients are the same, it is easy to make, does not require baking, and is irresistibly good. Generations of heartbroken, exam-weary teenagers have survived thanks to this cake. I serve it with pear or lemon sorbet, unsweetened cooked pears or a light vanilla-flavoured custard. Canned unsweetened chestnut purée is perfectly acceptable for this cake.

———————— Serves 6–8 ————————

8 oz (225 g) plain chocolate, chopped
8 oz (225 g) butter, softened
8 oz (225 g) unsweetened
 chestnut purée
8 oz (225 g) caster sugar

1–2 tablespoons rum

TO DECORATE
grated plain chocolate, or cocoa powder
 and icing sugar

Place the chocolate in a bowl then put the bowl over a saucepan of hot, not boiling, water and leave until the chocolate starts to melt. Stir the chocolate until it is smooth, then remove from the heat.

In another bowl, beat together all the remaining ingredients, except the grated chocolate or cocoa powder and icing sugar. Stir in the chocolate then spoon into a loaf tin or a ring mould. Cover and leave in the refrigerator overnight.

To serve dip the tin or mould briefly in hot water, place a plate over the tin or mould then, holding the tin or mould and the plate firmly together turn them over and give a sharp shake. Lift the tin or mould away. Sprinkle grated chocolate or cocoa powder and icing sugar over the top and serve sliced.

Variation

This cake, adorned with tiny meringue-mushrooms and marzipan pixies is sometimes served as a *Bûche de Noël*. One bite of it and anyone will believe in Father Christmas.

POIRES À LA FOURME D'AMBERT

Pears with blue cheese

Blue cheese has a great affinity with pears, which the charming Michel Mioche at the *Hotel Radio*, Chamalières, showed to good effect in a simple, elegant dessert containing one of the great cheeses of his native Auvergne, *Fourme d'Ambert*. This has quite a rich, tangy flavour and looks like a tall, slim Stilton. The other Auvergnat blue cheese, *bleu d'Auvergne*, or even Roquefort or Stilton can be used in place of *Fourme d'Ambert*. When selecting the pears, make sure that they have a good, definite taste – Comice and Williams are best – and that they are ripe. If you suspect the pears are not quite good enough, poach them before proceeding with the recipe.

Serves 6

3 large ripe pears
¹/₂ lemon
4 oz (100 g) caster sugar (optional)
6 slices brioche, each about ¹/₄ inch
  (5 mm) thick

8 oz (250 g) Fourme d'Ambert *or*
  any strong blue cheese, cut into
  6 slices
2 tablespoons pink or black
  peppercorns (optional)
1 tablespoon icing sugar (optional)

Peel the pears and rub them with the cut side of the lemon. If necessary, poach them in a saucepan which is just large enough to hold them, with the sugar and sufficient water to cover, until tender but not too soft. Halve, core and cut each pear into 8 slices.

Pre-heat the grill.

If you have a heart-shaped biscuit cutter, cut hearts from the brioche slices, otherwise, cut 6 circles. Cut the brioche trimmings into small cubes. Toast the brioche shapes until golden brown on both sides.

Scatter the brioche cubes evenly in 6 small gratin or small, shallow heatproof dishes. Place 4 slices of pear on top of the cubes then cover with a slice of cheese. Scatter over the peppercorns, if using. Place under the grill until the cheese has melted. Place a brioche heart or circle on top, sift over icing sugar, if using, and serve immediately.

OEUFS À LA NEIGE

Snow eggs

The most festive of desserts, a pile of snowball meringues floating on pale-yellow custard, *Oeufs à la neige* spells happiness at first sight.

———————— *Serves 4* ————————

FOR THE MERINGUES
4 egg whites
8 oz (225 g) caster sugar

FOR THE CUSTARD
1 pint (600 ml) milk
6 egg yolks
2 oz (50 g) caster sugar
2–3 tablespoons Grand Marnier, rum
  or orange flower water

TO SERVE
cocoa powder or
finely chopped candied orange peel or
grated plain chocolate or
caramel – 3 oz (75 g) caster sugar and
  2 tablespoons water and a few drops
  lemon juice

To make the 'snowball' meringues, bring a wide frying-pan or saucepan of salted water to the boil. Meanwhile, in a clean, dry bowl whisk the egg whites until stiff, but not dry. Gradually whisk in the sugar until stiff and shiny. Lower the heat beneath the pan so the water is barely simmering. Slide the egg whites, spoonful by spoonful on to the hot water but do not crowd them, and poach for 2–3 minutes depending on size, turning the balls over half-way through. Using a skimmer or slotted spoon, remove them from the water and place in a wide tray tilted gently, so they drain. You will have to cook the meringues in several batches.

Then on with the custard. Rinse a saucepan with cold water, leaving a few drops of water in the bottom to avoid scorching. Pour in the milk and bring quickly to the boil. Meanwhile, whisk the egg yolks and sugar until thick and pale yellow. Stir in a few spoonfuls of hot milk. Lower the heat beneath the saucepan then, using a wooden spoon, stir the egg yolk mixture into the pan. Continue to stir over a low heat until the custard is thick enough to leave a fine coating on the spoon; do not allow it to boil at any time. Remove the pan from the heat and leave the custard to cool, stirring occasionally. Add the Grand Marnier, rum or orange flower water.

When you are almost ready to serve, pile the meringues on each other. If you are in a hurry, sprinkle a little cocoa powder on top. If you have a minute, chop some candied peel or grate some plain chocolate and sprinkle over the meringues. If you have another 5 minutes, make a caramel by gently heating the sugar and water in a small heavy-bottomed saucepan for 2–3 minutes. Add the lemon juice and continue to heat until golden. Immediately remove from the heat and trickle in a criss-cross pattern over the meringues and the chocolate shavings; it will harden at once. Slide the pile of meringues into the centre of a wide shallow dish and pour the custard around, or serve the meringues and custard in separate bowls. This dish may be kept in the refrigerator for a day, but the caramel will melt.

Variation

The meringues may be served with a raspberry coulis, made by sieving 1 lb (450 g) fresh or frozen raspberries and sweetening to taste.

— THROUGHOUT FRANCE —

SALADE DE FRUITS

Fresh fruit salad

A fresh fruit salad is one of the most refreshing ways to end a meal; it is ideal after a *Coq au Vin* (see page 117) or a *Choucroute Garnie* (see page 148).

Choose a mixture of cherries, raspberries, peaches, apricots, pears, apples, plums, strawberries, figs, mangoes, melons, oranges, kumquats, tangerines, pineapple or bananas, according to availability. Then add blueberries, blackcurrants, redcurrants, grapes or fresh almonds as an accent. Serve in a single dish, individual bowls or glasses.

——————— *Serves 4* ———————

about 1¹/₄–1¹/₂ lb (550–750 g) fruit
juice 1 lemon
juice 2 oranges
4 tablespoons brandy, rum, kirsch,
  Cointreau or Grand Marnier
  (optional)
about 2–3 oz (50–75 g) sugar
3 oz (75 g) blueberries, blackcurrants,
  redcurrants or grapes, or
  2 oz (50 g) fresh almonds

TO SERVE
finely diced candied orange or
  grapefruit peel
finely chopped crystallised stem ginger
  or *fresh ginger*
small mint leaves
Tuiles *(see page 205)*

Peel and core or stone the fruit and half, slice or dice as appropriate. Place the fruit in a shallow dish, individual dishes or glasses. Pour over the lemon and orange juices and the brandy, rum, kirsch or liqueur, if using, and gently stir in sugar to taste. Cover the bowl and place in the refrigerator for at least 1 hour.

Just before serving, add blueberries, blackcurrants, redcurrants, grapes or nuts and scatter over candied orange or grapefruit peel, or ginger, or both, toss, sprinkle over small mint leaves and serve.

Variations

* For a special occasion, pour Champagne, or other sparkling white wine, over just before serving; do not toss but serve at once.
* Purée together 2 ripe peaches or 1 large mango, and the juice of 3 oranges then pour over the fruit.

— **THROUGHOUT FRANCE** —

COMPOTE DE FRUITS

Poached fresh fruit

This is a refreshing, light compote with clear, sharp fruit flavours. To make a good compote, you don't need exotic or perfect-looking fruit; fruit that is too ripe, not ripe enough, or too blemished to be acceptable in a basket of fresh fruit can be used. You can use just one type of fruit or a mixture but allow five to six pieces of fruit for four people.

The compote can be served in so many different ways, either lukewarm or cold: on plain yoghurt for breakfast, as a filling for *crêpes* and sweet omelettes, with *Gâteau Breton* (see page 218), *Kugelhopf* (see page 216), *Pain d'Épices* (see page 214) or warm *Madeleines* (see page 212).

——————— *Serves 4* ———————

1 lemon	*3 oz (75 g) green or black*
5–6 pears, peaches, apricots or apples,	*grapes (optional)*
or a mixture	*1 tablespoon brandy or*
2 oz (50 g) sugar	*Calvados (optional)*
10 fl oz (300 ml) water	*chopped mint, to serve (optional)*

Pare 2 × 3 inch (7.5 cm) strips of rind from the lemon, then squeeze the juice. Peel the fruit, cut in half and discard the cores or stones, as appropriate, then quarter or slice the fruit.

Put the lemon rind and juice, sugar and water in a medium saucepan, and bring to the boil. Add the fruit, lower the heat, cover and simmer gently for 8–15 minutes until just tender; turn the pieces over half-way through.

Remove the fruit with a slotted spoon and put in a shallow bowl to cool. Boil the cooking liquid until lightly thickened, then pour over the fruit. Add the grapes and brandy or Calvados if you wish. Cover and chill. Serve sprinkled with chopped mint leaves if you like.

POIRES, PRUNEAUX, ET ORANGES AU VIN ROUGE ET AUX ÉPICES

Pears, prunes and oranges cooked in red wine with spices

Serve with *Gâteau Breton* (see page 218), warm *Madeleines* (see page 212), *Pain d'Épices* (see page 214), or *Tuiles* (see page 205).

——————— *Serves 6* ———————

100 g (4 oz) plump raisins	*4 teaspoons black peppercorns*
6 large prunes, stoned	*pinch grated nutmeg*
1 lemon	*1 cinnamon stick*
3 oranges	*1 teaspoon coriander seeds*
6 firm but ripe pears with stems	*1 clove*
1 pint (600 ml) full-bodied red wine	*2 bay leaves*
6 oz (175 g) sugar	*1 tablespoon finely chopped fresh ginger*

Place the raisins and prunes in a bowl, pour over boiling water and leave for 1–2 hours. Using a potato peeler, pare 2 large strips of rind from the lemon and 1 of the oranges, then squeeze the juice from the lemon and orange. Finely grate the rind from 1 of the remaining oranges, then peel and thinly slice them both; reserve the grated rind and orange slices.

Peel the pears and place stem up, in a saucepan that they just fit. Add the wine, sugar, spices, bay leaves, strips of orange and lemon rind and the lemon and orange juices. Bring to the boil then cover, using a dome of foil if necessary to avoid crushing the pear stems, and simmer gently for 10 minutes. Drain the prunes and raisins, add to the saucepan and simmer for a further 15 minutes. Add the reserved orange slices, turn off the heat and leave the fruit to cool in the poaching liquid.

Transfer the prunes and raisins to a glass or china serving bowl and place the pears, stems up, on top. Put the orange slices round the edge.

Boil the poaching liquid over a high heat until slightly syrupy. Add the reserved grated orange rind and the ginger. Check the taste and add more ginger if needed. Discard the peppercorns, cinnamon, clove, orange and lemon rind. Leave the syrup to cool then pour, with the bay leaves, over the fruit. Serve when cold, or cover and refrigerate.

Opposite: POIRES, PRUNEAUX, ET ORANGES AU VIN ROUGE ET
AUX EPICES.

Variation

In Burgundy a few tablespoons of *crème de cassis* are often stirred into the wine syrup just before serving (if you do this, reduce the amount of sugar you add to the pears to about 4 oz (100 g)).

———————— **NORMANDY** ————————

SORBET AU CALVADOS

Calvados sorbet

Calvados is the brandy that is distilled from cider, in the same way as brandy is made from wine. This sorbet is a light and refreshing way of clearing the palate and digestion. It can also be served as a dessert with *Tuiles* (see page 205), in a large *Tulipe* (see *Tuiles*), with *Madeleines* (see page 212), or with a scoop of Chocolate Mousse (see page 184) and a tablespoonful of an apple Compote (see page 191).

———————— *Serves 4* ————————

6 oz (175 g) sugar
16 fl oz (575 ml) water
pared rind and juice 1 large lemon
½ egg white

2 tablespoons Calvados

FOR DECORATION
mint leaves

Gently heat the sugar and the water in a saucepan, stirring with a wooden spoon, until the sugar has dissolved. Add the lemon rind and bring to the boil. Boil hard for 2 minutes then cover and leave to cool.

Remove the lemon rind from the saucepan and strain in the lemon juice. Pour the liquid into a large ice-cube tray, then put in the freezer and leave for about 30 minutes until beginning to freeze at the edges.

Whisk the egg white until stiff. Tip the partially frozen mixture into a cold bowl and whisk briefly to break up the ice crystals. Add the Calvados and gently fold in the egg white using a cold metal spoon. Return to the ice-cube tray and place in the freezer and freeze until firm. Serve scooped into a cold bowl or individual glasses and decorate with mint leaves.

Opposite: SORBET AU CALVADOS with MADELEINES (*see page 212*).

CHARLOTTE AUX POIRES
Pear charlotte

Foods have highs and lows. Once upon a time no special Sunday lunch, no grand 'cousin Georges is back from Africa' dinner was complete without a Charlotte. These were extravaganzas of custard, gelatine, whipped cream and brandy encased in sponge fingers. They looked and tasted rich so cooks felt better people for serving them. Today fashions and tastes have changed. We want fresher flavours, we want textures, we shun gelatine, so the only Charlottes I serve now are packed with fruit, and the jacket is made of thin slices of bread. I use peaches, pears, apples or apricots for the filling and enhance the fruit flavour with lemon juice. The result is tangy, crunchy and utterly delicious whether it is served lukewarm or cold.

The secrets of a successful fruit Charlotte are cooking the fruit until it becomes very thick, filling the mould to the very top since during the cooking the fruit will settle, and using an apricot jam that is very sharp (add a little lemon juice if it is not). If the Charlotte becomes whimsical and does not unmould easily, don't complain, don't explain, don't panic; gather everything as well as possible, pour the warm apricot jam on top, sprinkle with a little icing sugar and serve your guests yourself. At the first bite, everyone will be conquered.

I serve the Charlotte with a light vanilla, or kirsch flavoured custard, or a raspberry or strawberry purée.

———————— *Serves 4* ————————

2 lb (1 kg) ripe pears
grated rind and juice 1 lemon
4 oz (100 g) unsalted butter
3 tablespoons apricot jam
8 slices firm bread, crusts removed

FOR THE GLAZE
2 tablespoons sieved apricot jam
1 tablespoon lemon juice

TO SERVE (optional)
icing sugar

Pre-heat the oven to gas mark 6, 400°F (200°C).

Peel, core and roughly chop the pears. Put into a heavy-bottomed saucepan, add the lemon rind and 1 oz (25 g) butter and cook over a low heat until the mixture is very thick. This may take between 20 and 35 minutes according to the quality of the fruit. Stir in the apricot jam and lemon juice.

Cut 2 circles from the bread, 1 to fit the bottom of a 6 inch (15 cm) charlotte mould and 1 for the top. Cut the remaining bread into strips. Melt the remaining butter then brush 1 side of each piece of bread completely with the butter. Line the mould with the bread (except the circle for the top), buttered side outwards and overlapping the pieces slightly to make sure there are no gaps.

Carefully pour the pear mixture into the mould; the mould should be filled to the top. Cover with the remaining bread, buttered side up. Bake for about 35 minutes until the top is crisp and brown. Allow the Charlotte to settle for 5–10 minutes after removing from the oven then place a plate on top and, holding the mould and plate firmly together, invert them, and give a sharp shake. Carefully lift off the mould.

For the glaze, gently heat the apricot jam and lemon juice together in a small saucepan until melted. Brush over the Charlotte. Sift over a little icing sugar, if liked, and serve warm.

Variations

* A handful of hazelnuts or raisins can be added to the pears just before stirring in the apricot jam, to provide extra texture, as well as flavour.
* To serve the Charlotte cold, unmould but do not glaze it. Leave it to cool completely then place in the refrigerator for about 4 hours. Brush with the glaze before serving.

*B*EIGNETS DE *P*OMMES AU *R*HUM

Apple fritters with raisins and rum

Raisins marinated in rum turn simple apple fritters into a sumptuous dessert. I like to serve *Compote de Fruits* (see page 191), red currant jelly and blackcurrant jelly, or a fruit sorbet with the fritters.

——————— *Serves 4* ———————

5 crisp apples
1¹/₂ oz (40 g) raisins
2 tablespoons rum
vegetable oil, for deep frying
caster sugar, for sprinkling

FOR THE BATTER
2 eggs, separated
3 fl oz (75 ml) light-flavoured beer
3 oz (75 g) flour
pinch salt
¹/₂ teaspoon groundnut oil
grated rind 1 lemon

Put the raisins in a bowl, stir in the rum and leave to stand for 2¹/₂ hours. Peel, core and thinly slice the apples, stir into the bowl and leave for about 30 minutes.

Meanwhile, make the batter. Slowly stir the egg yolks and beer into the flour and salt, then beat in the oil to make a smooth batter. Leave in a warm place for 1 hour.

Pre-heat the oven to gas mark 2, 300°F (150°C). Half fill a deep fat frying-pan with vegetable oil and heat to 375°F (190°C).

Drain the rum from the apples into the batter and stir in lightly. Whisk the egg whites until stiff but not dry then, using a large metal spoon, gently fold into the batter. Add the apples, raisins and lemon rind to the batter. Using a dessert spoon, scoop up individual slices of apple with a raisin or 2, and drop into the hot oil. Fry for about 3 minutes until golden on both sides, turning them over with a large spoon half-way through. Remove with a slotted spoon and drain on paper towels. Keep the fritters warm on plates lined with paper towels, in the warm oven. When all are cooked, sprinkle with caster sugar and serve warm.

OMELETTE AUX POMMES

Soufflé omelette filled with apples flavoured with rum

Whether filled with Fruit Compotes (see page 191), preserves or ice-cream, soufflé omelettes are easy to prepare, inexpensive and remain an unusual dessert. This light *Omelette aux Pommes* could be served with a bowl of soured cream or whipped cream.

———————— *Serves 4* ————————

2 crisp, firm, not too-sweet apples such as Granny Smith	*icing sugar, for sprinkling*
4 tablespoons dark rum	*TO SERVE*
3 oz (75 g) butter	*soured cream, or whipping*
5 eggs, separated	*cream, whipped*
2¹/₂ oz (70 g) caster sugar	

Peel and core the apples then cut into ¹/₄ inch (5 mm) thick slices. Place in a bowl, pour over the rum and leave for 1 hour.

Using a slotted spoon, remove the apple slices from the bowl. Melt 1¹/₂ oz (40 g) butter in a medium-size frying-pan, add the apple slices and cook over a low heat for 10 minutes, turning the slices over half-way through this time.

In a bowl, whisk together the egg yolks, sugar and rum marinade until frothy. In another, clean, dry bowl, whisk the egg whites until stiff but not dry. Gently fold into the egg yolk mixture.

Melt half of the remaining butter in a 7 inch (18 cm) omelette pan over moderate heat. Pour in half of the egg mixture. Cook for 5 minutes. Hold a plate over the pan, invert the omelette on to the plate, then slide it back into the pan for a further 2 minutes. Slide the omelette on to a warm serving plate. Repeat with the remaining egg mixture.

Place half of the cooked apples in the centre of each omelette and fold the omelette over them. Sprinkle the tops with icing sugar and serve at once with soured cream or whipped cream.

*F*LANS *C*ARAMEL

Caramel custards

These light, caramel-coated custards are one of the quickest, easiest, inexpensive of desserts, yet remain one of the most popular. *Flans Caramels* can be kept for 1–2 hours in an oven with the heat turned off and served lukewarm for the lightest, most exquisite texture. They can also be cooked in advance and refrigerated, but they must be returned to room temperature at least 30–45 minutes before serving as they should never be served cold. However, refrigerating the custards does tend to make them more compact.

For a special occasion, serve a platter with a variety of *Flans Caramel* and *Mousse au Chocolat* (see page 184), and *Tuiles* (see page 205) or warm *Madeleines* (see page 212).

——————— *Serves 4* ———————

$2^1/_2$ oz (75 g) sugar
2 eggs, beaten
2 egg yolks
1 pint (600 ml) milk
1 tablespoon finely chopped candied
  orange peel, or very finely grated
  fresh orange rind (optional)

FOR THE CARAMEL
3 oz (75 g) sugar
1 tablespoon water
$^1/_4$ oz (7 g) butter

Pre-heat the oven to gas mark 4, 350°F (180°C).

To make the caramel, gently heat the sugar and water in a small, heavy-bottomed saucepan, swirling the pan, until the sugar has dissolved. Bring to the boil, then lower the heat and leave to develop an amber colour; do not stir. Immediately remove from the heat, swirl in the butter then quickly pour into individual heatproof dishes. Without delay, turn the dishes in all directions so the caramel coats the bottoms and sides before it hardens. Leave to cool.

Whisk the sugar, eggs and egg yolks together until pale.

Pour the milk into a heavy-bottomed saucepan previously rinsed with cold water and bring to the boil. Slowly pour into the eggs, stirring constantly, then pour into the dishes.

Place the dishes in a large baking tin and pour in hot water to come half-way up the sides of the dishes. Bake for 20 minutes, until lightly set in the centre.

Remove the baking tin from the oven and lift the dishes from the water. Sprinkle candied orange peel or grated orange rind on top of each custard, if you wish.

Variation

If you would like to unmould the custards, cook for another 5 minutes. Remove the dishes from the baking tin and leave for a few minutes. Run a knife round the edges of the dishes and place a flat plate on top of each dish. One at a time, hold each dish and plate firmly together and give a decisive shake so the custard slides from the dish.

— **THROUGHOUT FRANCE** —

SOUFFLÉ AU CHOCOLAT

Chocolate soufflé

A soufflé spells luxury, excitement and happiness yet this superstar is very easy to make. There is a base which gives flavour, and whisked egg whites for lightness and drama. Cooking for the right length of time in a pre-heated oven is important.

I like to serve the Soufflé with a bowl of whipped cream or, for a lighter, fresher dessert, a dish of sliced pears or peaches sprinkled with lemon juice.

———— *Serves 4–6* ————

3¹/₂ oz (90 g) plain chocolate, chopped
2 oz (50 g) caster sugar, plus extra for coating
2 tablespoons plain flour
8 fl oz (250 ml) milk

¹/₂ oz (15 g) butter
3 whole eggs, separated
1 extra egg white
2 tablespoons strong coffee
icing sugar, for dusting

Pre-heat the oven to gas mark 6, 400°F (200°C). Butter a 7 inch (18 cm) soufflé dish then sprinkle caster sugar in an even layer over the bottom and around the sides.

Place the chocolate in a heatproof bowl, and place the bowl over a saucepan of hot water. Cover the bowl and leave the chocolate to melt, stirring twice.

Meanwhile, stir the flour and 3 tablespoons milk together in a bowl. Bring the remaining milk to the boil in a heavy-bottomed saucepan then slowly stir into the bowl. Pour back into the saucepan and cook over a medium heat, stirring constantly, until the sauce boils and thickens. Simmer for 2–3 minutes. Remove from the heat, add the butter and leave to cool for a few minutes. Stir in the yolks one at a time, then stir in the chocolate mixture and the coffee.

In a clean, dry bowl, whisk the egg whites until you see soft peaks standing in the bowl, then gradually whisk in the sugar until you have shiny firm peaks and all the sugar is absorbed. Slowly pour the chocolate mixture all around the edges of the bowl and fold the two mixtures together, lifting delicately but quickly using a tablespoon.

Pour into the soufflé dish, run the point of a knife around the edge of the mixture then place the dish in the oven. Lower the temperature to gas mark 4, 350°F (180°C). After 45 minutes gently open the oven door and pull the soufflé towards you, quickly dust the top with icing sugar. Slide the dish back into the oven and bake for a further 5 minutes. By then the soufflé will have puffed up and browned, and be lightly set in the centre.

As soon as the soufflé is ready take it to the table. Plunge 2 large spoons straight down into the soufflé in one decisive move to break the crust before you serve it.

–––––––– BURGUNDY ––––––––

LE SABLÉ
AUX POMMES ET AUX CASSIS

Rich shortbread biscuits with apples, and blackcurrant sauce

Today, ambitious young chefs search and try, and search and try new ways to serve dishes which suit current tastes yet remain close to the traditional cooking of their area.

One of the most successful in this quest is Bernard Loiseau, chef-patron of one of France's most celebrated three-star restaurants in Burgundy, the *Côte d'Or*, in Saulieu. This is one of his recipes, which he cooked for me and it was very, very good.

———————— *Serves 4* ————————

FOR THE BISCUITS
6 oz (175 g) plain flour
4 oz (100 g) unsalted butter, diced
2 oz (50 g) icing sugar
1 egg yolk

FOR THE APPLE
1 large apple, peeled and diced
1/2 oz (15 g) unsalted butter
2 tablespoons sugar
8 walnut halves

FOR THE BLACKCURRANT SAUCE
1 pint (600 ml) red wine
2 tablespoons crème de cassis
2 oz (50 g) sugar
5 oz (150 g) fresh or frozen
  blackcurrants (optional)

To make the biscuits, place the flour in a bowl, add the pieces of butter, sugar and half of the egg yolk. Using your fingertips, mix together lightly for a few minutes, then turn on to a lightly floured surface, form into a ball then knead by pushing portions of the dough away from you with the heel of your hand. Gather the dough into a ball again then repeat for 1–2 minutes. Cover and place in the refrigerator for 30 minutes.

To make the blackcurrant sauce, bring the wine to the boil with the *crème de cassis* then add the sugar. Simmer for 15 minutes or until reduced by just over half. Add the blackcurrants, if using, and simmer gently for 3–4 minutes. Keep aside for later.

Pre-heat the oven to gas mark 5, 375°F (190°C).

Roll out the dough on a lightly floured surface using a lightly floured rolling pin until it is very thin. Using a 3 inch (7.5 cm) fluted biscuit cutter or a wide glass, stamp out 8 circles. Carefully transfer to a baking sheet. Using the point of a sharp knife, mark a lattice pattern on the top of 4 circles. Beat the remaining half egg yolk and brush over the top of the marked circles to glaze. Bake for about 7 minutes until lightly browned. Leave to cool briefly before transferring to a wire rack to cool completely.

For the apple, heat the butter in a small frying-pan, add the apple and cook, stirring occasionally, for about 4 minutes. Sprinkle over the sugar, add the nuts, stir and sauté for 1 minute.

Divide the blackcurrant sauce between 4 dessert plates. Place an unglazed biscuit in the centre of each plate, then top with apple and walnuts. Cover with a glazed biscuit to make a pretty golden sandwich on a pool of blackcurrant.

*T*ARTE AUX *Q*UETSCHES

Plum tart

Purple *quetsches* are Alsace's favourite cooking plum. They can be bought raw, cooked, dried and lately frozen, and can be used in a variety of desserts, including many different versions of *tarte aux quetsches*. This is my favourite recipe because it is light and allows the sharp, clear flavour of the fruit to stand out better.

Be sure to place the halved plums cut side up so the juices do not make pastry soggy.

Serves 6

FOR THE PÂTE SUCRÉE (SWEET PASTRY)
6 oz (175 g) plain flour
pinch salt
3¹/₂ oz (90 g) unsalted butter, softened
    and diced
2 large egg yolks
2 oz (50 g) caster sugar

FOR THE FILLING
4 fl oz (120 ml) milk

4 fl oz (120 ml) double cream
¹/₂ vanilla pod
3 eggs
about 3 oz (75 g) caster sugar,
    depending on the sharpness of the
    plums
¹/₂ teaspoon plain flour
1¹/₄ lb/550 g quetsch, or other sharp
    but well-flavoured plums, halved
    and stoned
caster or icing sugar, for sprinkling

To make the pastry, butter a 9 inch (23 cm) fluted flan tin, about 1 inch (2.5 cm) high, and preferably loose-bottomed.

Sift the flour and salt on to the work surface and form a well in the centre. Put the butter, sugar and egg yolks into the well, then, using your fingertips, lightly 'peck' these ingredients together until they resemble coarse scrambled eggs. Still using the fingers, gradually draw in the flour until large crumbs are formed. Using a pastry scraper or metal palette knife, quickly gather the crumbs to form a ball and knead gently by pushing the dough away from you with the heel of one hand, then gathering up the dough with the pastry scraper or palette knife and repeating for a minute or so until the dough peels easily away from the work surface. Form into a ball, wrap in cling film and place in the refrigerator for 30 minutes.

On a lightly floured surface and using a lightly floured rolling pin, roll out the pastry to a circle about 11 inches (23 cm) in diameter. Fold the pastry backwards over the rolling pin, then lift it and lay it centrally over the flan tin. Lift the edge of the pastry and gently ease it into the shape of the tin, making sure it fits well into the flutes and the angle between the base and the sides. Roll the pin firmly over the top to remove surplus pastry, then, with your finger, press the dough evenly up the sides. Use your finger and thumb to neatly crimp the edge. Prick the base lightly with a fork and place the pastry case in the refrigerator for at least 15 minutes until firm.

Pre-heat the oven to gas mark 7, 425°F (220°C). Lay a sheet of greaseproof paper in the base of the pastry case and cover with baking beans. Bake in the oven for about 12 minutes, then carefully lift away the greaseproof paper and baking beans. Return the pastry to the oven and bake for a further 3–4 minutes. Remove from the oven. Lower the oven temperature to gas mark 6, 400°F (200°C).

For the filling, pour the milk and cream into a saucepan, add the vanilla pod and bring to the boil.

Whisk the eggs and sugar together until light and frothy, then quickly whisk in the flour. Remove the vanilla pod from the saucepan. Slowly pour the boiling liquids on to the egg yolk mixture, whisking constantly, to make a smooth custard. Leave to cool, stirring occasionally to prevent a skin forming.

Arrange the plums, cut-side uppermost, in the base of the pastry case then pour the custard around them. Place in the oven and bake for about 20–25 minutes until lightly set in the centre, and golden brown.

Transfer the flan tin to a cooling rack and leave until the tart is lukewarm. Remove the outer ring of the tin if a loose bottomed tin has been used, sprinkle the filling with caster or icing sugar and serve the tart, preferably while it is still warm.

*T*ARTE AUX *P*RUNEAUX

Prune tart

Throughout France, prunes are used in a variety of savoury as well as sweet dishes, but this tart is one of the most delectable sweet recipes I know.

———————— *Serves 4* ————————

4 oz (100 g) plain flour
pinch salt
2 oz (50 g) unsalted butter, softened
cold water
icing sugar, for sprinkling

FOR THE FILLING
12 oz (350 g) large prunes
4 tablespoons apricot jam
4 teaspoons cognac, prune brandy or
  armagnac

Soak the prunes in tea or water for at least 2 hours.

Place the flour and salt in a bowl, toss in the butter then rub into the flour until the mixture resembles breadcrumbs. Rapidly stir in the water to make a soft but not sticky dough and form into a ball. Cover, and place in the refrigerator for 30 minutes.

Pre-heat the oven to gas mark 6, 400°F (200°C). Butter an 8 inch (20 cm) flan tin.

Drain the prunes and remove the stones. Put the prunes into a bowl, crush them coarsely with a fork, then mix in the apricot preserve and half the brandy.

Roll out the dough on a lightly floured surface to a circle about 10 inches (25 cm) in diameter. Fold the dough back over the rolling pin and carefully transfer to the flan tin. Pass the rolling pin over the flan tin to remove excess pastry. Prick the base with the tip of a knife or a fork.

Spread the prune mixture in the pastry shell and bake for about 35–40 minutes.

Remove the tart from the oven and transfer to a wire rack. Sprinkle with the remaining brandy and leave to cool slightly. Sprinkle with icing sugar just before serving warm or lukewarm.

— **THROUGHOUT FRANCE** —

*T*UILES

Crisp almond biscuits

These delicate biscuits shaped like dainty tiles have always been popular, but lately the same mixture has been used to make cup-shaped *tulipes* and *aumonières* (children's purses), which are filled with ice cream, sorbets or diced fresh fruit. Pine nuts can be used instead of almonds.

———— *Makes about 30* ————

4 oz (100 g) flaked almonds	4 oz (100 g) caster sugar
2 oz (50 g) blanched whole almonds	2 egg whites
2 oz (50 g) butter at room temperature	2 oz (50 g) plain flour
	pinch salt

Pre-heat the grill. Place all the almonds under the grill and toast for a few minutes, stirring frequently, until evenly browned. Leave to cool then crush the flaked almonds and cut the whole almonds into slivers.

Cream the butter and sugar until the mixture is light and fluffy. Stir in the egg whites and blend well. Lightly stir in the flour, crushed almonds and salt to make a mixture that is very soft. Cover and leave in the refrigerator for 1–1½ hours.

Pre-heat the oven to gas mark 6, 400°F (200°C). Butter 2 large baking sheets and oil a rolling pin.

Drop teaspoons of the almond mixture on 1 baking sheet, spacing them well apart. Flatten lightly with a fork dipped in cold milk, then sprinkle with the slivered almonds. Lower the oven temperature to gas mark 5, 375°F (190°C), and bake for 5–8 minutes until the edges turn light brown. Meanwhile, fill the second baking sheet in the same way.

To make *Tulipes*, mould the warm biscuits around a small orange, or around the base of a small bowl.

Immediately the biscuits are removed from the oven, lift them one at a time from the baking sheet with a spatula, and quickly roll around the rolling pin to shape it. If the biscuits cool and harden before you have shaped them, return to the oven for a few minutes to soften. Bake the second batch while the first are being shaped. Continue in this way until all the mixture has been cooked. Leave to cool on wire racks or on a cold surface. When cold, store in an air-tight container for up to 1 week.

TARTE TATIN

Warm caramelised apple upside-down tart

The two *demoiselles* Tatin who ran the *Hôtel Terminus* in Lamotte-Beuvron near the Loire river had both determination and imagination. One version of the legend behind their famous tart is that one day, by mistake, one of the sisters put the apples she had cooked for a tart into the dish before she had lined it with pastry. Instead of tipping the apples out and starting again, she put the pastry on top and inverted the tart after cooking. The alternative story is that similar upside-down tarts had been made for years throughout France but the sisters' version must have been especially good and because their customers included many travellers and people who were visiting the area for the excellent hunting, the fame and reputation of their tart quickly spread. There is a rumour that 'Maxim's', the temple of chic cookery in Paris, sent a spy disguised as a gardener to Lamotte-Beuvron to learn their 'secret'.

Nowadays, pears only or a mixture of pears, apples and sometimes quinces often replace the plain apples used in the original recipe.

I have prepared this splendid tart many times and like to serve it with well chilled, lightly sweetened whipped cream. Sometimes I add chopped crystallised ginger, grated lemon rind, rum, Calvados, Cognac or Grand Marnier to the cream.

Serves 6

FOR THE PASTRY
5 oz (150 g) plain flour
1¹/₂ tablespoons caster sugar
1 teaspoon salt
3 oz (75 g) butter, chilled
2 tablespoons vegetable oil
3–5 tablespoons cold water

FOR THE FILLING
3 lb (1.5 kg) firm apples, such as
    Granny Smith or 1 lb (450 g)
    apples and 1¹/₂ lb (750 g) ripe but
    firm Comice pears

3 oz (75 g) unsalted butter
6 oz (175 g) sugar
juice 2 lemons
finely grated rind 1 lemon

TO SERVE
lightly sweetened whipped
    cream, chilled

Place the flour, sugar and salt in a large bowl. Toss in the butter then rub into the flour until the mixture resembles coarse sand. Rapidly stir in the oil and cold water and press into a ball. Place on a floured work surface, then pressing the dough with the heel of your hand, push a little at a time away from you in a quick motion. When all the ingredients are well blended, gather the dough into a ball and knead for 1 second. Sprinkle with flour, wrap in cling film and place in the refrigerator for about 40 minutes to become firm.

Pre-heat the oven to gas mark 7, 425°F (220°C). Butter a 9 inch (23 cm) loose-bottomed cake tin.

For the filling, peel, core and quarter the apples. Heat the butter in a thick-bottomed frying-pan, add the sugar and stir with a wooden spoon for about 3 minutes until it bubbles and becomes golden. Pack the apples into the pan, sprinkle with lemon juice and lemon rind and cook over a high heat, for about 20 minutes, shaking the pan occasionally, until the fruit is a rich golden colour, and rendered most of its juices. Transfer to the cake tin.

Remove the pastry from the refrigerator, place it on a floured work surface and beat it with a rolling pin if it is too hard to handle. Knead it for a few minutes then form into a ball. Place a rolling pin in the centre of the ball and roll back and forth firmly. Lift the dough, turn it once and continue rolling until you have a circle about 11 inches (28 cm) in diameter. Fold the dough back over the rolling pin, lift it carefully then unroll it over the cooked apples. Tuck the edge of the dough between the fruit and the side of the dish. With the tip of a knife cut a few holes in the dough so the steam can escape.

Place the tart in the oven and bake for about 30 minutes, until the pastry turns brown. Place a wide plate on top of the tart, hold the edges of the tin and the plate firmly together then quickly turn the tart upside down. Give a sharp punch on the bottom of the tin with the palm of your hand covered with an oven glove, and let the tart unmould itself slowly. Serve warm with the sweetened cream.

Note

A *Tarte Tatin* that has been cooked but not unmoulded can be reheated in an oven pre-heated to gas mark 5, 375°F (190°C) for about 10 minutes. If it has been unmoulded, place it under a hot grill until the topping is bubbling and the fruit warm. Of course, neither will be as good as a freshly baked tart.

TARTE AU CITRON
ET À L'ORANGE

Lemon, orange and almond tart

Topped with pieces of fruit, *Tarte au Citron* has a refreshing texture and flavour, and the combination of crisp pastry shell and light, sharp custard topped by a layer of orange and lemon pieces covered with marmalade and toasted almonds is irresistible.

———————— *Serves 8* ————————

FOR THE PASTRY
6 oz (175 g) plain flour
3¹/₂ oz (90 g) butter
2 egg yolks
pinch of salt
3 oz (75 g) icing sugar
2 tablespoons very cold water

FOR THE FILLING
3 lemons
2 oranges
3 oz (75 g) caster sugar
2¹/₂ oz (70 g) unsalted butter
2 eggs
4 tablespoons sieved orange marmalade
1 oz (25 g) flaked almonds
icing sugar, for dusting

Sift the flour on to the work surface and form a well in the centre. Place the butter, egg yolks, salt, sugar and water in the well and gradually work in the flour using the fingertips to make a soft dough; add a little flour if it is too sticky or add a little water if it is too dry. Form the dough into a ball. Push the dough away from you with the heel of one hand. Gather it up again using a metal palette knife or pastry scraper and repeat for 1–2 minutes. Form into a ball, cover and chill for 45 minutes.

Pre-heat the oven to gas mark 6, 400°F (200°C). Butter a 9 inch (23 cm) loose-bottomed flan tin.

Using a rolling pin, flatten the dough, then roll it out to a circle about 11 inches (27 cm) in diameter. Fold the dough back over the rolling pin and carefully lift it over the flan tin. Press the dough into the shape of the tin, allowing the excess to hang over the rim. Pass the rolling

Opposite: TARTE AU CITRON ET A L'ORANGE.

pin across the top of the rim to cut off the dough neatly. With the thumb of one hand, push the edge of the pastry inwards gently, then, with a finger of the other hand, pinch the pastry pushed up initially to crimp it. Continue around the edge of the pastry shell. Prick the bottom of the pastry shell with a fork. Place in the refrigerator for 15–30 minutes.

Lower the oven temperature to gas mark 5, 375°F (190°C). Line the pastry shell with greaseproof paper, fill with baking beans and place the flan tin on a baking sheet. Bake for 15 minutes, until set and lightly browned. Remove the baking beans and greaseproof paper and bake the pastry for a further 5 minutes. Leave to cool.

Grate the rind from 1 of the lemons and ¹/₂ an orange. Squeeze the juice from 2 lemons. Beat together the sugar, butter and orange and lemon rinds until light and fluffy, then gradually beat in the eggs. Slowly stir in the lemon juice.

Peel both oranges and the remaining lemon as you would in order to eat them, then using a sharp knife carefully scrape off the pith. Holding the fruit over a bowl to catch any drips, cut down between the membrane and the fruit to remove the segments. Add any juice collected in the bowl to the butter mixture then spread in the pastry case. Place the lemon and orange segments on top, pressing them down lightly.

Warm the marmalade in a small saucepan over a low heat. Carefully brush over the orange and lemon segments then sprinkle with the almonds. Bake for 15 minutes. Leave to cool for 10 minutes then transfer to a wire rack to cool completely. Dust with icing sugar just before serving the tart.

Opposite: Provence – Here, everyone tries to grow their own herbs.

CHOUX À LA CRÈME
Choux buns with pastry cream filling

Lovers call each other *mon petit chou*, mothers call their babies *mon chou à la crème*. Choux pastry is probably France's most beloved pastry. It may be served plain, without a filling or topping, when it will be *chouquette* in Paris and *bijoux* (jewels) in Provence, or it may be filled with pastry cream (*crème patissière*), whipped cream, or a mixture of the two, as in this recipe, or with ice-cream.

Small balls of choux pastry covered with hot chocolate sauce are called *profiteroles*; if the pastry is shaped like tiny cabbages it is a *chou*; if the pastry is finger-shaped it becomes an *éclair*; if cooked in a large ring a *Gâteau Paris Brest*; little choux puffs piled in conical shape on a sweet pastry base and stuck together with caramel, make a spectacular *Croquembouche*.

Unfilled choux pastry shapes can be kept in an air-tight container in a cool place or the refrigerator, frozen for about 1 month. Defrost in the refrigerator for 24 hours. If necessary, crisp-up the choux pastry in the oven before serving. Always allow to cool before filling. Choux pastry shapes filled with ice-cream or cream must be served at once, but if pastry cream has been used they can be kept for a little while.

—— *Makes 30–35 small buns* ——

FOR THE CHOUX PASTRY
9 oz (250 ml) mixed milk and water
1 teaspoon sugar
pinch salt
3 oz (75 g) unsalted butter, diced
5 oz (150 g) plain flour
4 eggs, beaten
1 egg beaten with 1 teaspoon water, to glaze

FOR THE PASTRY CREAM FILLING
(CRÈME PATISSIÈRE)
6 egg yolks
4 oz (100 g) sugar

1¹/₂ oz (40 g) plain flour
pinch salt
15 fl oz (450 ml) milk
1–2 tablespoons brandy, kirsch, Grand Marnier, rum or orange flower water
¹/₂ oz (15 g) unsalted butter
2 fl oz (50 ml) double or whipping cream, whipped (optional)

TO FINISH
sifted icing sugar

Pre-heat the oven to gas mark 6, 400°F (200°C). Butter 2 baking sheets.

To make the choux pastry, pour the milk, water, sugar, salt and butter into a saucepan. Heat gently until the butter melts then bring quickly to the boil. Remove from the heat and quickly add all the flour in one go. Beat very vigorously with a wooden spoon for 1 minute then return the pan to a moderate heat and stir until the dough comes away from the sides of the pan. Leave to cool slightly then beat in the eggs a little at a time, making sure all the egg has been incorporated before adding any more. Continue adding egg until the mixture is thick, smooth and glossy. Place teaspoonfuls of the mixture, spaced well apart, on the baking sheets, and brush the tops with the egg glaze.

Bake for about 10 minutes, then increase the oven temperature to gas mark 7, 425°F (220°C) and bake for a further 15–20 minutes until well-risen, golden and crisp. Pierce a small hole in the bottom of each bun to allow the steam to escape then return to the oven with the heat switched OFF and the door propped open with a wooden spoon, for a few minutes so the pastry dries inside. Transfer to a wire rack to cool.

To make the filling, whisk the egg yolks and sugar together until thick and pale yellow, then stir in the flour and salt. Bring the milk to the boil in a heavy-bottomed saucepan previously rinsed with cold water, then slowly pour into the egg yolk mixture, stirring constantly. Pour back into the pan and cook over a low heat, stirring constantly, until the mixture thickens. Continue to cook, still stirring, for 2 minutes but do not allow to boil. Remove from the heat and stir in the brandy, kirsch, Grand Marnier, rum or orange flower water, and the butter. Leave to cool, stirring occasionally to prevent a skin forming. If you want to make the filling a little lighter, gently fold in the whipped cream if using, when the pastry cream is cold.

Increase the size of the hole in the bottom of each choux bun with the tip of a sharp knife then either pipe, or use a small spoon to fill them with the pastry cream. Sprinkle the tops with icing sugar.

MADELEINES

Madeleine cakes

These delicate, shell-shaped cakes evoke nostalgic memories for most French people and are associated with leisurely moments. Madeleines have never been out of fashion, but today we tend to serve them luke-warm because this is when they taste best and are at their most moist, with just the right touch of crispiness around the edges. There is also a trend, especially in restaurants, to make them in different sizes with a variety of flavours added, such as pistachio nuts, almonds, honeys, jams or chocolate. But, in spite of all the renewed attention to their plump selves, Madeleines remain steadfastly part of Sunday *goûters* (afternoon teas), dinners and picnics, served with cooked fruit, Chocolate Mousse (see page 184), sorbets or just a glass of chilled sweet wine or a flute of Champagne. Madeleines are also what we put in the pockets of our brave four year olds when they start kindergarten, to remind them there is life beyond such hardship.

Madeleines are baked in special shell-shaped tins and I have found that 3 inch (7.5 cm) ones produce the best results. The cakes are often flavoured with orange flower water; lemon is also a popular flavouring, and I add another one by browning the butter. They are baked at a high temperature so the traditional dome will form.

———— *Makes about 20 cakes* ————

3¹/₂ (90 g) unsalted butter, diced
3 eggs, separated
3¹/₂ oz (90 g) caster sugar
3¹/₂ oz (90 g) plain flour
scant teaspoon baking powder
grated rind 1 large lemon
1¹/₂ tablespoons lemon juice
pinch salt
icing sugar, for dusting

TO SERVE
a bowl of sliced oranges marinated in
    orange liqueur and a little
    lemon juice
a bowl of Fruit Compote (see page 191)
a bowl of Mousse au Chocolat
    (see page 184)
a bowl of whipped cream flavoured
    with diced crystallised ginger

Heat the butter in a small saucepan until it turns brown. Remove from the heat and cool slightly. Whisk the egg yolks and sugar together until pale yellow and thick, then slowly stir in the melted butter.

Whisk the egg whites until stiff but not dry. Using a large metal spoon, fold the egg whites, spoonful by spoonful, into the yolk mixture, alternating with spoonfuls of flour and the baking powder and salt. Finally, gently fold in the lemon rind and juice. Refrigerate the mixture for about 30 minutes.

Meanwhile, pre-heat the oven to gas mark 7, 425°F (220°C). Butter and flour the Madeleine moulds thoroughly.

Spoon the cake mixture into the moulds so they are two-thirds full then bake for about 7 minutes, until domed, then lower the oven temperature to gas mark 5, 375°F (190°C) and bake for a further 7 minutes or so until pale golden brown on top and slightly darker brown around the edges.

Run the tip of a knife around the edge of each Madeleine and unmould on to a wire rack. Dust with icing sugar and serve lukewarm.

Note

* Madeleines can be kept in an air-tight container for 2–3 days, or in a freezer for 1 month.

* To warm Madeleines for serving, place them on a baking sheet, cover lightly with foil and re-heat in an oven pre-heated to gas mark 4, 350°F (180°C) for 5–8 minutes.

PAIN D' EPICES

Spice bread

Both returning Crusaders and merchants trading in the Middle East and the Orient are credited with introducing *Pains d'Epices* to France. Many regions developed their own versions, and Burgundy was no exception. From the fourteenth century the recipe developed in Dijon was considered the best in the dukedom and was served at the court as a festive dessert. It was (and still is) also believed to have therapeutic properties. By the eighteenth century egg yolks, rye flour, richly flavoured honey and 10 spices were declared compulsory. Today, *Pains d'Epices* may be made with wheat flour, which gives a lighter, softer, crumbly texture, or rye flour, which produces a more dense, heavy cake, or a combination of the two flours. The mixture may be flavoured with just lemon and aniseed, or with many other spices such as cloves, coriander and cinnamon.

Pain d'Epices remains a beloved cake in Burgundy. It may be sold as a pretty crown decorated with candied fruits, or as iced fancy shapes, such as donkeys, fish, pigs, rabbits or hearts, often with initials on the icing. *Nonnettes*, once prepared in convents, hence the name, and *Duchesses* are small *pains d'épices* filled with blackcurrant jelly, apricot, quince, plum or tangerine jam, and covered with a thin layer of icing or chocolate. Made as a 15 lb (6.75 kg) loaf called *pavé d'épice de santé*, 'health cake', it is thinly sliced and lightly buttered as part of the afternoon tea or the children's *goûter* when they return home from school. Dipped into a glass of sweetened red wine it is served as a tonic to the elderly and the sick. With the current popularity of sweet-savoury flavour combinations it is served in thin, toasted slices with goose or duck liver. *Pain d'Epices* may also replace bread or sponge fingers as a lining for a charlotte, and it can be blended with a rich custard to make a delicious ice cream, or combined with cream, rum and raisins to become a traditional pudding.

─────────── *Serves 6–8* ───────────

8 oz (225 g) fragrant honey	*2 tablespoons finely diced candied*
4 fl oz (120 ml) water	*orange peel*
10 oz (300 g) light rye flour	*2 teaspoons baking powder*
1 teaspoon coriander seeds, crushed	*2 egg yolks*
¹/₂ teaspoon ground cinnamon	*2 teaspoons milk*
1 tablespoon aniseeds, chopped	
¹/₂ teaspoon ground cloves	*TO SERVE*
1 teaspoon grated nutmeg	*warm, poached peaches or pears, ice*
finely grated rind and juice 1 lemon	*cream or custard*

Gently heat together the honey and water, stirring until the honey has melted. Remove from the heat. In a mixing bowl stir together the flour, spices, lemon rind and candied orange peel, then slowly pour in the honey and water, stirring constantly. Beat in the lemon juice, cover and leave at room temperature for 2 hours.

Pre-heat the oven to gas mark 2, 300°F (150°C). Generously butter an approximately 8 × 4 (20 × 10 cm) loaf tin.

Stir together the baking powder and egg yolks then stir into the cake mixture, which should be very soft and smooth; add a little water to soften it if necessary. Pour the cake mixture into the loaf tin and bake for 1 hour. Transfer the loaf to a wire rack, brush the top with milk and leave to cool. Wrap tightly in greaseproof paper and foil and leave for 3 days to allow the flavour to develop. Always keep the cake tightly wrapped as it is quite dry and quickly dries out further if left unwrapped. Serve sliced with warm poached peaches or pears, ice cream, or custard.

Variations

* In Alsace, *Pains d'Epices* are spicy biscuits which are baked in many different fancy shapes and decorated with coloured icings. They are hung on Christmas trees, included in children's Christmas stockings or given as presents, with initials piped on them.

KUGELHOPF

Rich yeast cake with sultanas

In Ribeauville, they make splendid hand-printed fabrics, they have geranium-covered balconies, beautiful timber houses and a splendid bell-tower. But the town is most well-known for its annual festival celebrating Alsace's most beloved cake – *Kugelhopf*. During the festival there are horse drawn carriages, little girls with wide red skirts, and huge red or black bows on their heads, men wearing black felt hats, black trousers and red jackets, joyful sounds of bells ringing and brass bands playing and everywhere streets lined with tables covered with piles of *Kugelhopf* cakes, both large and small, all equally golden, plump and fragrant. I thought I had eaten my share of this cake in Colmar's beautiful baker's shop, *Helmstetter*, and Strasbourg's splendid pastry shop, *Christian*, comparing the flavour of the fresh, sweet *Kugelhopf* with the more buttery taste of traditional French brioches. But in Ribeauville we had an absolute *Kugelhopf* orgy. At breakfast, lunch, tea and dinner we ate *Kugelhopf*. By the end of the day we felt like Walking *Kugelhopfs* ourselves – and we probably looked like them too.

The name comes from *Kugel*, which means a ball, and *hopf*, the name for beer yeast. *Kugelhopfs* can be either slightly sweet and flavoured with almonds and raisins, or slightly salty with streaky bacon. *Kugelhopfs* are baked in fluted brown, glazed earthenware ring moulds, which make them look like a medieval merchant's hat. Metal moulds will do if you cannot find the real thing, but earthenware does give more even baking. The flavour of *Kugelhopfs* develops if they are baked a day in advance. They also freeze well.

Serves 8

4 oz (100 g) sultanas	3 eggs, beaten
3 tablespoons kirsch or rum	5 fl oz (150 ml) warm milk
13 oz (400 g) strong plain flour	6 oz (175 g) unsalted butter, softened
1 packet easy-blend yeast	4 oz (100 g) almonds, slivered
pinch of salt	caster sugar, for sprinkling
3 oz (75 g) sugar	icing sugar, for dusting

Put the sultanas into a bowl, stir in the kirsch or rum and leave to marinate while making the dough.

Put the flour into a bowl, stir in the yeast, salt and sugar then make a well in the centre. Pour the eggs into the well and start drawing the flour mixture into the eggs, and gradually pour in the milk. Work all the ingredients together to make a smooth dough then beat until it comes away from the sides of the bowl. Turn on to a lightly floured surface and knead for 10–15 minutes, stretching the dough with your hands, until it becomes very elastic. Lightly work in the butter. Place the dough in an oiled bowl, cover with a damp towel, and leave to rise for 2 hours at room temperature until doubled in volume.

Butter a 9–10 inch (23–25 cm) fluted ring mould, strew it with the almonds and sprinkle with a little caster sugar.

Turn the dough on to a floured surface, punch it down, and stretch it a few times with your hands. Drain the sultanas then knead briefly into the dough. Place in the mould and leave to rise to the top of the mould – about 1 hour.

Pre-heat the oven to gas mark 6, 400°F (200°C).

Bake the *kugelhopf* for 40–45 minutes until well-browned and a skewer inserted in the centre comes out clean. If the top becomes too brown cover with foil and lower the temperature to gas mark 4, 350°F (180°C). Remove from the oven, allow to cool for a few minutes then turn on to a wire rack to cool completely. Dust liberally with icing sugar.

Variation

Serve sprinkled with kirsch or rum and topped with whipped cream or with fruit compôte.

Note

To use dried yeast measure 4 tablespoons lukewarm milk into a small bowl, stir in 1 teaspoon of the sugar, sprinkle over 4 teaspoons dried yeast, stir once and leave until there is a good head of froth, about 10–15 minutes. Pour into the flour with the eggs. Use only 3 fl oz (75 ml) milk for the recipe.

To use fresh yeast, heat the milk in the recipe until it is lukewarm, pour into a small bowl and crumble over $1^1/4$ oz (35 g) fresh yeast, stir together with a teaspoon then add to the flour after the eggs, as instructed for the milk.

——————— **BRITTANY** ———————

GÂTEAU BRETON

Butter cake

What gives all Breton pastries and cakes their unique flavour is the mixture of sugar and good quality, fresh, lightly salted butter that is used to make them. This Breton cake seems everyone's favourite at tea time or after a light meal, when it is served with cooked fruits, such as *Compote de Fruits* (see page 191) or Pears Cooked in Red Wine (see page 192).

This recipe was given to me by one of Brittany's superwomen, Madame Sylvie Kersabiec. She runs the large manor house that has been in her family for ten centuries, is the elected mayor of her village, Moustoir-ac, helps with her husband and son's flock of sheep, smokes two packets of *Gitanes* a day and is an attentive grandmother of eight. Quite appropriately, her family motto is *Mieux vaut penser que rire* – it's more worthwhile to think than to laugh.

——————— *Serves 6–8* ———————

6 egg yolks, lightly beaten
2 teaspoons milk
9 oz (275 g) plain flour

6 oz (175 g) caster sugar
7 oz (200 g) lightly salted butter,
diced

Pre-heat the oven to gas mark 4, 350°F (180°C). Butter a 9 inch (23 cm) springform cake tin or loose-bottomed flan tin.

Place about half an egg yolk in a small bowl and mix with the milk. Reserve for later. Put the flour into a large bowl, stir in the sugar then form a well in the centre. Add the butter and remaining egg yolks. Using your finger tips mix them together, then work in the flour to make a smooth, but sticky, dough.

Sprinkle your hands with flour. Place the dough in the tin or ring and pat it out to fill the tin or ring. Using a fork, score criss-cross lines on the top, brush with the egg yolk and milk mixture then bake for about 1 hour until firm to the touch. Cool slightly, then carefully transfer to a wire rack.

Variation

Layer thinly sliced raw apple or stoned and chopped, cooked prunes between two layers of the cake mixture before baking.

INDEX